Hospitality English

Han ChunYoung Lee KeumSil Oh SunYoung

Hotel & Restaurant

파워북

Table of Contents

Preface

Hospitality English is written to empower you and help you on your way to become a future leader of hospitality industry, especially in the hotel and restaurant fields.

With vivid pictures and film scripts, you can learn essential english structures for such common functions as welcoming guests, taking a reservation, taking a meal order, and dealing with problems.

This textbook will give students the opportunity to build confidence and improve fluency. While you learning new words, phrases and sentences in this text book you can learn Hospitality English easier and faster than you have ever studied.

This text book has been divided into 2 parts:

Part 1. At Hotel
Part 2. In the Restaurants

And each chapter deals with vivid situations and contains

- Dialogues
- Vocabulary
- Activities
- Film script
- Other materials

Part I. At Hotel

Chapter 1. Taking a Reservation

Unit 1. Taking a Reservation by Phone

R: Reception, **C**: Caller

Dialogue 1

R : Good Morning, Intercontinental Hotel.
May Lee Speaking.
How can I help you?

C : Good Morning. I'd like to make a room reservation for tomorrow night, please.

R : Yes, sir. Could I have your name, please?

C : Paul. Paul Belchamber.

R : Would you prefer a single or a double room?

C : Double room, please.

R : Smoking or non-smoking?

C : Smoking, please.

R: Reception, **C**: Caller

Dialogue 2

R : The London Hilton, Lyons Speaking.
May I help you?

C : I'd like to book a double room for tonight, please.

R : Yes, sir. May I have you name, please?

C : Gillian. Gillian White.

R : How do you spell your name, madam?

C : G-I-L-L-I-A-N for Gillian and W-H-I-T-E for White.

R: Reservation, C: Caller

Dialogue 3

R : Good morning, reservations. Park speaking.
Can I help you?

C : Hello, I'd like to reserve a room for me and my daughter, please.
Do you have a double room for next Thursday?

R : Yes, we do. How many nights is it for?

C : Two. Thursday and Friday.

R : Yes, we can do that.

C : OK. I'll take it.

R : I'll need your name and a credit card number.

C : Suzan Martin. M-A-R-T-I-N. I have a Visa.
9876-5432-1234

R : And what's the name on the card, please?

C : My own name. It's my name.

R : OK. And could you just tell me the expiry date?

C : It expires August 2010.

R : That's fine. Your reservation number is H-A-D, 110, 7 double 2, 123.

C : ...double 2, 123.

R : We look forward to seeing you next Thursday...
Thanks for calling.

C : Thank you. Bye.

R : Goodbye.

Vocabulary

- book(= *reserve*)
- make a reservation
- a single (*double, twin, suite*) room
- credit card
- spell
- available
- expire
- look forward to

Activities

※ *Make a request with* ***Can*** *or* ***Could*** *and work with a partner.*

Example make / a room reservation
Could I *make a room reservation*?

1. help / you

2. have / your name

3. book / a double room

※ *Make a request with* ***I'd like to*** *and work with a partner.*

Example book / a single room
I'd like to book a single room.

1. reserve / a parking space

2. speak to / the manager

3. make / a reservation

Type of rooms and beds

twin

single

double

suite

Credit Cards

- card number
- valid from date
- expiration date

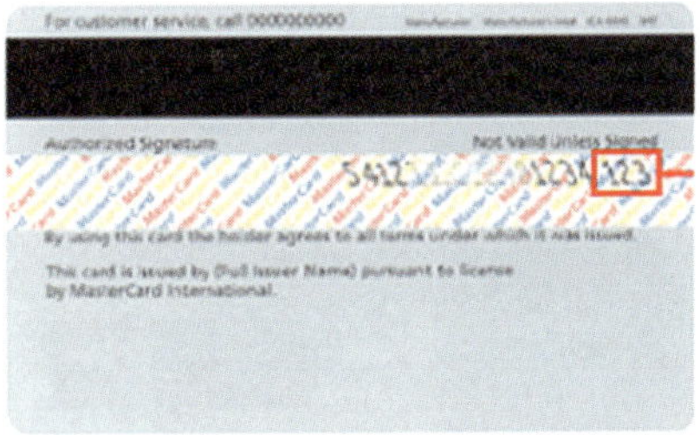

- issue number
- signature
- security code

Unit 2. Taking a Reservation by Email

Reservation by email - example 1

To: book@hayatt seoul.com
From: Tim@hotmail.com
Subject: Room Reservation

Dear Sir,

I'd like to reserve double rooms with twin beds, for five nights from Monday 6th October for me and my wife, and our 2 children ages 5 and 7.

If possible, we'd like bathrooms with a shower and bath. Also please book me a table for four in the restaurant for the Monday evening at 7:30.

We will arrive mid-afternoon.

Regards
Tim Parsons

Email 용어

- To : 수신인
- From : 발신인
- CC(Carbon Copy) : 참조
- BCC(Blind Carbon Copy) : 숨은 참조
- Attachment : 첨부 파일
- Subject : 제목

Reservation by email - example 2

To: book@hayatt seoul.com
From: Tim@hotmail.com
Subject: [RE]: Room Reservation

Dear Tim Parsons

We reserved your reservation of a double and an adjoining twin room for 5 nights from 6th to 10th October. A table for four is reserved in the restaurant for dinner at 7.30.

We look forward to seeing you and your family on Monday 6th October.

Regards
Robert Parker
Reservations

Email Etiquette

- Salutation: 인사는 필수요건이다.
- Personal Questions : 개인적 질문은 삼간다.
- Simple Sentences : 단순 명쾌한 문장으로 작성한다.
- Polite Expression : 예의바른 표현을 사용한다.

■ Reservation by email - example 3

To: book@holiday.com
From: lks@btms.co.kr
Subject: Reservation for Lee, Keumsil from 23rd - 29th Room Reservation

Dear Sir

I have booked the following dates with you over the phone : 23rd – 29th inclusive(7 nights)

I understand that the total cost of $210.00 is to be paid in advance by credit card. I look forward to arriving at your hotel around 1:30 pm on 23rd September.

Thank you for your time, and if there are any issues regarding this booking, please contact me by my email.

Kind regards,
Keum Sil, Lee

Vocabulary

- adjoining room
- a single (*twin, double*) bed
- bathroom
- bath
- book a table
- restaurant
- mid-afternoon
- confirm
- details
- accommodation
- issue
- in advance
- contact
- regards

Activities

※ *Write an email for making a reservation with the following information.*

1. Hotel Plaza : Two double rooms for April 5th with bathrooms with shower, non-smoking room.

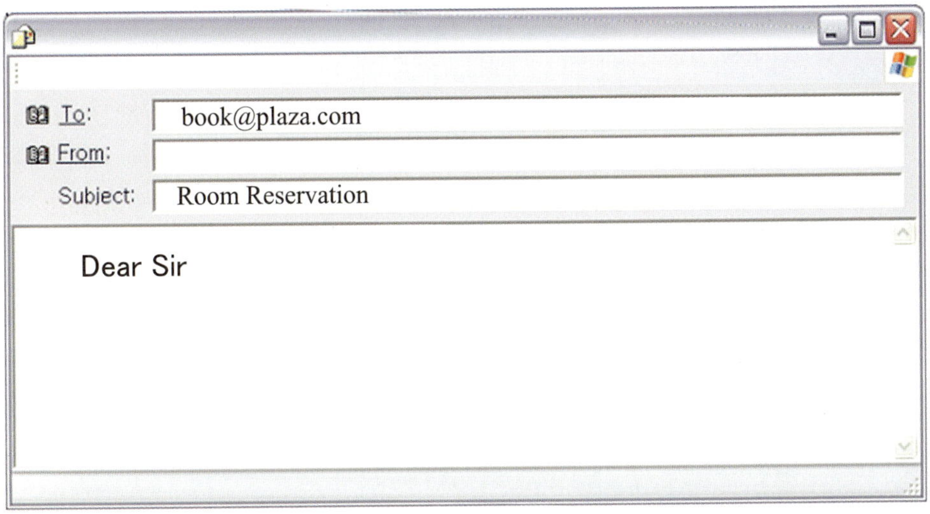

2. Hotel Antoinette : A single room for 2 nights with a double bed.

■ 영화로 배워보는 Hospitality English (1) - Home Alone 2

Kevin: Excuse me, where's the lobby?

Passenger: Down the hall and to the left.

Kevin: Thanks.

Kevin: Wow.

Kevin: I'll do just that. Howdy-do. This is Peter McCallister, The father. I'd like a hotel room, please. With an extra-large bed, a TV... and one of those little refrigerators you have to open with a key. Credit card? You got it.

Reservation Clerk: Plaza Hotel Reservations, may I help you?

Kevin: Howdy-do. This is Peter McCallister, The father.

Reservation Clerk: Yes, sir.

Kevin: I'd like a hotel room, please. With an extra-large bed, a TV... and one of those little refrigerators you have to open with a key.

Reservation Clerk: Yes, you'll need a major credit card upon check-in.

Kevin: Credit card? You got it.

Reservation Clerk: Thank you. Enjoy your stay.

■ 영화로 배워보는 Hospitality English (2) - 1408

Operator: Good evening, Dolphin Hotel. How might I direct your call?

Mike: Yeah, hi. I'm calling about room 1408.

Operator: One moment please, sir.

Man: How may I help you?

Mike: Yeah, I'd like to stay in room 1408 please.

Man: That room is unavailable, sir.

Mike: I didn't tell you which date. How about Saturday?

Man: It's unavailable.

Mike: (*laughs*) The following Tuesday?

Man: Unavailable.

Mike: Next month?

Man: Unavailable.

Mike: Next summer?

Man: (*hangs up*)

Chapter 2. Checking In

Unit 1. Welcoming a Guest

Dialogue 1

R: Reception, **G**: Guest

R : Welcome to the Queen's Hotel.
G : I'd like to check in, please. I have a reservation.
My name is Paul Belchamber.
R : Could I have your confirmation number, Mr. Belchamber?
G : My confirmation number is H-R-D 1234.
(*A receptionist entered his confirmation number into a computer*.)
R : I have you down for 4 nights. Is that right?
G : Yes.
R : And that's a non-smoking room.

Dialogue 2

R: Reception, **G**: Guest

R : Good afternoon, sir. May I help you?
G : Good afternoon. My name is Paul Lyons. I'd like to check in, please. I have a reservation for a double room.
R : Yes, Mr. Lyons, let me see. Yes, today and tomorrow, the 7th and 8th of June. Could you please fill in this registration card?
G : Yes, of course. Do I fill in my home address?
R : Yes, please. And could I have your passport?...
Thank you. Your room number is 761. It's on the 7th floor. And here's your key card for your room. Would you like to have a dinner in the restaurant this evening?
G : Yes, please. Can you reserve me a table for 2 at seven o'clock?
R : Certainly. The bellman will help you with your luggage.
G : Thank you.
R : My pleasure, Mr. Lyons. Enjoy your stay.

R: Reception, G: Guest

Dialogue 3

R : Sorry to keep you waiting, Sir.
G : Do you have any vacancies for tonight?
R : I'm sorry, sir. We're fully booked until this weekend.
G : Oh, that's too bad.
R : We have rooms available from next Tuesday.
G : OK. Good bye.

Vocabulary

- check in
- have a reservation
- confirmation
- non-smoking room
- fill in(= *out*)
- registration card
- passport
- room number
- have dinner(*lunch, something to eat, ..., etc.*)
- porter
- luggage(=*baggage*)
- vacancy

Activities

※ *Work with a partner and read and make a dialogue with the following information. Student A is a receptionist at the Antoinette Hotel. Check in the guests.*
(Remember these things : name, address, passport, key card, registration card.)

Example Receptionist : Good afternoon. How can I help you?
Guest : Good afternoon. My name is Jeong Ho-Jong. I'd like to check in, please.

1. Name : Mr Slone / Mrs Slone
   Room : double, three nights
   Address : 66 Hight st. upon Thames Kingston
   Passport No : 125000432

2. Name : Mr. Jeong / Mrs. Lee
   Room : double, cradle, two nights
   Address : Twin Bldg. 275-4 Yangjae-Dong, Seocho-Gu, Seoul
   Passport No : 876578999

Registration card (숙박등록카드)

Hotel　REGISTRATION CARD　Hotel

NAME　NATIONALITY

ADDRESS

CITY OR TOWN　CAR REGISTRATION NO.

DATE OF ARRIVAL　DATE OF DEPARTURE

METHOD OF PAYMENT　☐ C. Card　☐ Cash　☐ Cheque

ROOM RATE　☐ DINNER, BED & BREAKFAST　☐ BED & BREAKFAST

NEWSPAPER ORDERED　CHECKOUT TIME 10am

SIGNATURE　ROOM NO

Notes: *Cheques must be accompanied by a current BANK card.*
Credit Cards must be imprinted and signed, amount to be verified prior to departure
Cash customers can elect to either pay in advance, or on a day to day basis.
(prior to 12 noon each day for the following days stay).

[registration card sample]

More words to use

- name
- nationality
- city or town
- car registration no.(number)
- date of arrival
- date of departure
- method of payment
- room rate
- B&B (=Bed & Breakfast)
- signature
- room no.(number)

세계 각국의 여권

More words to use

- passport
- surname
- given name
- nationality
- date of birth
- date of issue
- date of expire
- authority

Unit 2. Filling Out a Registration Form

■ Sample 1

Registration Card

Name	: Mr. Paul Lyons
Address	: 66 high street upon Thames,
Passport number	: EP000119
Arrival date	: 07/06/2008
Departure date	: 08/06/2008
Room number	: 761
Signature	: *Park S.J*

■ Sample 2

Registration Card

Family name	: Rodriguez
First name	: Michelle
Date of birth	: Feb. 14th, 1979
Address	: 321 E Kitty Hawk Dr.
City : Midwest city	**State** : Oklahoma **Zip** : 73110
Home phone	: 230-123-9876
Car license plate No.	: N/A
Signature	: *D.Beckham*

- registration
- family name
  (= *surname, last name*)
- first name(=*given name*)
- car license plate
- zip = zip code
  (=*postal code*)
- N/A = not applicable
- signature

Activities

※ *Work with a partner. Student A is a receptionist at the 'A' Hotel. And Student B is a guest of the 'A' hotel. Make a sentence for each item and fill out a registration card with a guest's information.*

Example Name
→ *Could I have your name, please?*

Registration Card

- Name
- Address
- Passport number
- Arrival date
- Departure date
- Room number
- Signature

Unit 3. Explaining a Room to a Guest?

B: Bellman, **G**: Guest

Dialogue 1

(*A bellman opened the door.*)

B : After you, ma'am.

G : Thanks.

(*A bellman unloaded the bags from the trolley and placed them near the luggage stand. Then he pulled the drapes open.*)

B : This thermostat controls the room temperature. To make the room cooler, press this "down" button.

G : Actually, the room is a bit warm. Can you give it more air conditioning?

B : Sure.

(*A bellman turned up the air conditioning.*)

G : Thank you.

B: Bellhop, **G**: Guest

Dialogue 2

(*A bellhop opened the door.*)

B : After you, sir.

G : Thank you.

B : Here is the minibar. Drinks and some snacks are available for purchase. The price list is on this card.

(*A bellhop pointed out the coffee maker.*)

B : And here's the self-serve coffee maker. It's complimentary, of course.

(*Then he opened the closet door.*)

B : You'll find extra pillows and blankets here if you need them.

G : OK.. Lovely.

B : To use this safe, follow the instructions on the door. Please secure your valuables here whenever you leave the room.

B : All right. Those are the basics. Can I answer any questions for you?

G : No, not now. I think I have it.

B : Well, if you have any questions at all later on, please don't hesitate to call the front desk.

G : Thanks.

B: Bellman, G: Guest

Dialogue 3

G : How can I find out when things like the fitness center are open?

B : Channel 2 on your TV gives some information. And a more thorough list is in this hotel-information folder.

G : All right.

B : If you have any questions during your stay, the concierge would be happy to answer them.

Vocabulary

- unload
- trolley
- luggage stand
- drapes (=*curtains*)
- thermostat
- air conditioning
- purchase
- minibar
- coffee maker
- complimentary
- pillow
- blanket
- safe
- instruction
- secure
- valuables
- basics
- closet
- concierge
- hesitate

Activities

※ *Match these **facilities and services** with the icons.*

air conditioning	(　　)	gymnasium	(　　)
baby sitting	(　　)	hair dryer	(　　)
beauty parlour	(　　)	internet	(　　)
boutique	(　　)	jacuzzi	(　　)
car park	(　　)	laundry service	(　　)
conference facilities	(　　)	minibar	(　　)
safe box	(　　)	outdoor	(　　)
direct dial telephone	(　　)	swimming pool	(　　)
pay TV	(　　)	room service	(　　)
radio	(　　)	wake-up call	(　　)
restaurant	(　　)	sauna	(　　)
satellite TV	(　　)	sea view	(　　)

■ 영화로 배워보는 Hospitality English (3) - 1408

Woman : Welcome to the Dolphin, sir. Are you checking in?
Mike : Mike Enslin. One night.
Woman : And how are we spelling that today?
E-N-S-L-I-N? E-N-S-L-I-N.

'NOTES : ALERT MANAGEMENT BEFORE CHECKING GUEST IN'

Mike : Yeah.
Woman : Uh, would you excuse me for a moment, sir?
Mike : Sure.
Woman : Mr. Dempsey, Mike Enslin's just checked in.
Mr. Dempsey : Where is he?
Woman : He's over at my desk.
Mr. Dempsey : That's fine, Marie. I'll take care of it.
Woman : Okay. It'll just be a minute, Mr. Enslin.

영화로 배워보는 Hospitality English (4) - Home Alone2

Kevin : Hi.

Desk Clerk : Can I help you?

Kevin : Reservation for McCallister.

Desk Clerk : A reservation for yourself?

Kevin : Ma'am, my feet are hardly touching the ground. I'm barely able to look over this counter. How can I make a reservation for a hotel room? Think about it.

: A kid going into a hotel... making a reservation... I don't think so.

Desk Clerk : I'm confused.

Kevin : I'm travelling with my dad. He's on business. He's at a meeting. I hate meetings. Plus I'm not allowed to go in only to sit in the lobby. That's boring.

Kevin : So my dad dropped me off here. Gave me his credit card and said whoever was checking people in... to let me in the hotel room so I won't get into mischief. And ma'am, sometimes I do get into mischief...We all do!

Chapter 3. Hotel Services

Unit 1. Concierge Services(1)

C: Concierge, G: Guest

Dialogue 1

G : Excuse me. How do I find room 103?

C : Take the lift to the first floor.
Turn left when you come out of the lift, walk along the corridor and it's on the left.

C: Concierge, G: Guest

Dialogue 2

G : Hi. Where is the hair salon, please?

C : It's in the basement. Go through the door past the exchange bureau and down the stairs.
Go along the corridor and turn right.
And the hair salon is in front of you.

G : Thanks.

C : You're welcome.

Dialogue 3

C: Concierge, **G**: Guest

G : Hi. Can you tell me where I can change some Euro dollars?
C : Yes, there's an exchange bureau in the foyer.
G : Do you know if it's open now?
C : Yes, it's open from 8:00 a.m. to 11:00 p.m. every day.
G : Great. And I need to change my plane ticket.
C : There's a travel agent next to the hotel.
It's open from 9:00 a.m. to 5:00 p.m.
G : And I'd like coffee. Is there a coffee shop around here?
C : Yes, the coffee shop's over there behind the lift.
It's open 24 hours a day.
G : The lifts? You mean the elevators?
C : Yes, that's right. Behind the elevators.

Vocabulary

- take
- walk along
- basement
- go through
- past
- exchange bureau
- corridor
- turn (*right, left*)
- foyer
- open
- travel agent
- lift (=*elevator*)
- mean
- behind

Activities

※ *Use **the prepositions** to describe what you see in this picture of a room. Some examples are given.*

Example The vase is *on* the table.
There is a table *in front of* sofa.

• above	• on	• in the corner	• between
• under	• next to	• in front of	• behind
• on the left / right		• near	• in

※ *Complete these sentences with **the correct preposition**.*

• off	• outside	• on	• across
• straight on	• towards	• up	• over

1. Turn right and walk ________ the big hotel.
2. Take the second left. Go ________ and then turn right.
3. Go ________ the bridge and ________ the hill.
4. Park the car ________ the bank.
5. You get on the train at Rossio and get ________ at Oriente.
6. Go ________ the road and the cinema is ________ your right.

■ How to Read Wine Label

<French Wine Label>

<Italian Wine Label>

1. Type of wine / 2. Wine appellation / 3. Additional denomination
4. Vintage year / 5. Name of the wine / 6. Color of the wine
7. Quantity in milliliters / 8. Alcohol content by volume
9. Nation of origin (in our case, obviously Italy)
10. Bottling company data
11. Importer (this information is obviously missing from labels of Italian wines purchased in Italy).

Unit 2. Concierge Services(2)

C: Concierge, G: Guest

Dialogue 1

G : Hi. Do you have a list of good restaurants near here?
C : Certainly, sir.
G : I was thinking of an Italian place.
C : OK. There is a very good one within 5-minute walk from here, sir.

C: Concierge, G: Guest

Dialogue 2

G : I need to go downtown. I think I should take a taxi.
C : What time would you like to arrive downtown, Mrs. Martin?
G : At about 7 o'clock.
C : OK. I'll book one for you at 6:30.

Dialogue 3

C: Concierge, G: Guest

C : Concierge.

G : Hello. We need to find a baby sitter tonight for our daughter.

C : We have a free child care center—our Kid's Club—until 7:30 in the evening.

G : Yes, I heard about that from the front desk. But I'm afraid we'll be out much later, from 6:00 to about 10:00.

C : Then perhaps one of on-call child care workers would be available. Let me check... Yes, we have several on-call people available tonight. Would you like to book someone from 6 until 10?

G : Are they dependable? What qualifications do they have?

C : They have to have a license from the state to work for us, sir. They are very good. And these child care workers charge $10, but the guest and the hotel split that. You would pay $5 an hour, and the hotel would match it.

G : Sounds good. Could you send the sitter up to Room 1235 by six? We need someone to stay until 10 or 10:30.

C : Right. We'll arrange for a sitter to come to Room 1235 at 6.00 and we'll specify that the job might last as late as 10:30.

G : Perfect. Thank you.

Vocabulary

- on foot (*by bus* / *car* / *train* / *air*)
- downtown
- baby sitter
- free child care center
- afraid
- license
- state
- charge
- split
- match
- stay
- arrange
- specify

Activities

※ *Respond to the requests using* ***one, some, another*** *or* ***some more****. And practice the requests and responses with a partner.*

Example **A** Could we have *some* bread? (get / some)
B Yes, I'll *get* (you) *some.*

1. Can I have an orange juice, please? (get / one)

2. Is the exchange bureau open? I need some change. (get/some)

3. My bath towel is very wet. (get / another)

4. This fork is dirty. (bring / another)

5. There isn't enough soap in the bathroom. (bring / some more)

Concierge

Stay knowledge about local attractions and services by reading local newspapers, checking relevant web-sites, and maintaining connections with service providers.

Unit 3. Housekeeping Services

Dialogue 1

H: Housekeeping, **G**: Guest

H : Housekeeping. Marisa speaking. Can I help you?

G : Yes, please. My husband's suit needs dry cleaning and I have a dress that needs ironing. Shall I leave them at reception?

H : No, you don't need to do that. I'll send someone up for them right away. What's your room number?

Dialogue 2

H: Housekeeping, **G**: Guest

G : Hello, this is Mr. Jang in Room 4321. I'd like to need extra pillows and a complimentary toothbrush.

H : All right, sir. I'll be right there.

H: Housekeeping, G: Guest

Dialogue 3

H : Good morning, house keeping. Can I help you?

G : Yes, please. Can you put a new zip in a pair of trousers? I need them this afternoon.

H : We can do that for you by lunchtime, sir. Do they need pressing?

G : Oh... yes, please.

H : I'll send someone up to your room.

Vocabulary

- housekeeping
- suit
- dry cleaning
- ironing (=*pressing*)
- extra
- toothbrush
- zip
- a pair of
- trousers
- send up

※ *Look at the examples. And complete these sentences with* ***need(s) or don't/doesn't need.***

Activities

Example
- He *needs* his trousers this afternoon.
- Her dress *needs* ironing
- We *need to have* them this afternoon.

1. The rooms ____________ cleaning after each guest leaves the rooms.

2. The room maids ________ to change the towels every day.

3. Your jacket _____________ ironing.

4. The guest in room 1021 _____________ a taxi now.

5. No, thank you. We _____________ a porter.

6. You ___________ to pay now, sir. I'll put it on your bill.

Unit 4. Room Services

R: Room service, G: Guest

Dialogue 1

R : Good morning. Room service.

G : Good morning. Could we have a continental breakfast for two? With orange juice and coffee, please.

R : Certainly. A continental for two. Which room number, please?

G : 567. How long will it be? We need to leave in half an hour.

R : It'll be with you in fifteen minutes.

G : Great. Thank you very much.

R: Room service, G: Guest

Dialogue 2

R : Room service, can I help you?

G : Hello, could I have a bottle of champagne, please?

R : Certainly, what room number, please?

G : Room 237.

R : And how many glasses do you need?

G : We need three, please.

R : Right away, sir.

R: Room service, G: Guest

Dialogue 3

R : Room service, how may I help you?
G : Hello. This is Nancy Drew in room 567.
R : I'd like a Caesar salad, please.
G : Certainly ma'am. A large salad or just a side salad?
R : A large salad, please. Large enough to be a dinner in itself.
G : Right. A large Caesar salad.
R : Would you like anything else, ma'am?
Some wine perhaps? Or some other beverage?
G : I'll just have some mineral water, please.
R : Thank you, ma'am. That will be $12.35 with tax. Your meal should reach you in about 30 minutes.

Vocabulary

- room service
- continental breakfast
- a bottle of
- champagne
- glass
- side
- beverage
- mineral water
- reach
- with tax (=*tax included*)

Activities

※*Use **some** or **any** in the following sentences.*

Example Can we have *some* water, please?
I don't want *any* butter on my toast.

1. Do you have ________ decaffeinated tea?

2. I want ________ milk with my crackers.

3. Is there ________ carrot cake left?

4. Would you like ________ fresh ground pepper on that salad?

5. Have ________ sweet potatoes.

6. Are there ________ rooms with a view of the ocean?

7. There are ________ clean towels in the closet.

8. Are there ________ hangers in the closet?

9. Could I have ________ ice please?

10. Do you have ________ low fat desserts?

Unit 5. For Business Travellers

Dialogue 1

R: Reception, **G**: Guest

G : We're planning a conference for one thousand people in Seoul. Can you tell me a little about your conference facilities?

R : Certainly. We have a total of 28 meeting rooms. The theater-style room is the largest and holds 1,200 people, then there's the boardroom-style, and finally the classroom-style which is the smallest. The 19th floor has a rooftop banqueting room with panoramic views of the city.

G : Fine. What about audio-visual equipment?

R : We can organize digital projectors, slide projectors and screens, Power Point facilities....

G : Good. And what about business services?

R : We have high-speed data lines, and full secretarial services, and we can also arrange video conference facilities for you.

G : Excellent. Can you send me your information pack? I'll contact you next week.

Dialogue 2

R: Reception, G: Guest

G : Can you tell me about your in-room facilities?

R : Of course. All rooms have satellite TV with pay-per-view facilities so that you can watch films, play games, and listen to music. There's internet access for sending e-mails, accessing website, and finding out information about the hotel, for example, services, facilities and car hire. We have 24-hour room service and laundry service...

G : What about facilities for business travellers?

R : All rooms have multi-line phones. But printer, photocopier, and fax are in the business center just opposite the reception. The center is fully equipped and offers broadband internet access.

Vocabulary

- conference
- facility
- meeting room
- theater
- hold
- boardroom
- rooftop
- banqueting
- panoramic
- audio-visual
- equipment
- organize
- projector
- high-speed
- secretarial
- arrange
- pack
- contact
- in-room
- satellite TV
- pay-per-view
- access
- car hire
- standard
- business traveller
- photocopier
- equip
- offer
- broadband
- video conference

※ *Look at the examples. And use* ***both... and, so,*** *or* ***but*** *to link these pairs of sentences.*

1. The hair salon is open during the week.
   It's closed at weekends.

   ____

2. The restaurant is fully booked.
   We can't take any more bookings.

   ____

3. The hotel has a fitness center.
   The leisure center has a fitness center.

   ____

4. The table was booked for eight o'clock.
   The guests didn't arrive until 9.00.

   ____

※ *Look at the pictures and match the words.*

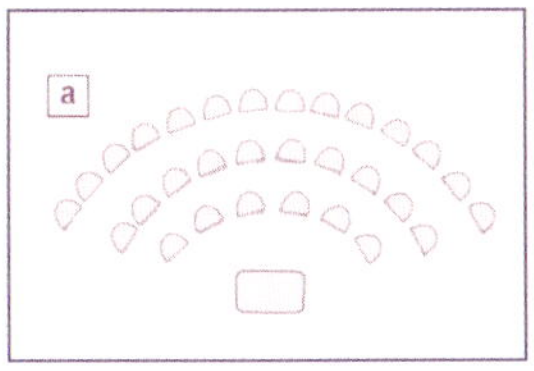

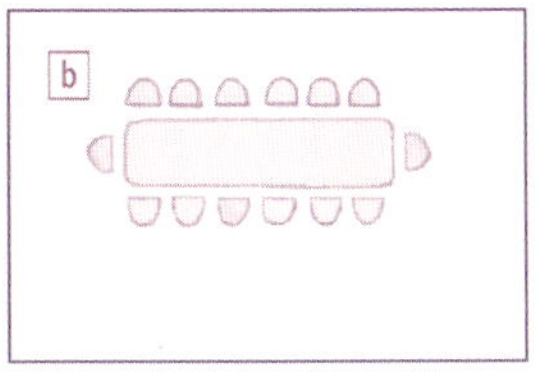

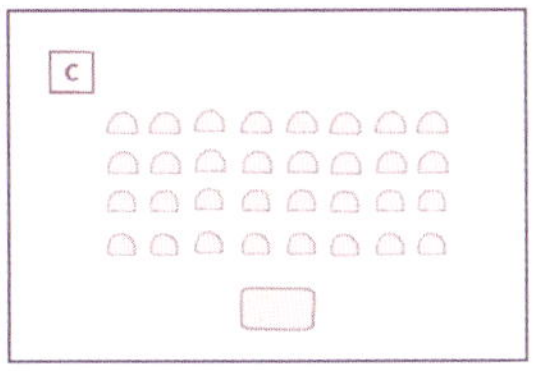

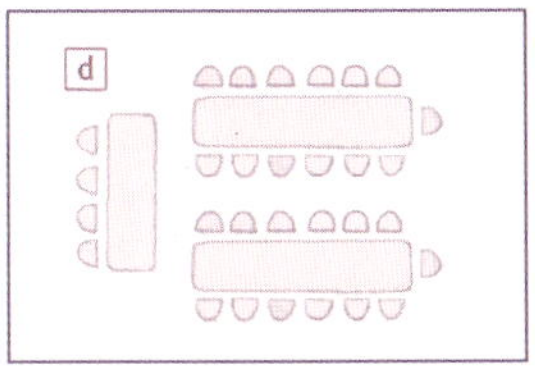

- boardroom-style meeting room
- theater-style meeting room
- banqueting room
- classroom-style meeting room

Mr. Thomas: Excuse me, miss. May I help you?
Vivian: I'm going to my room.
Mr. Thomas: Uh, do you have a key?
Vivian: Oh, I forgot that cardboard thing. I'm on the top floor.
Mr. Thomas: You're a guest here?
Vivian: I'm ... I'm with a friend.
Mr. Thomas: And who would that be?
Vivian: Edward...
Mr. Thomas: Edward?
Vivian: Edward... Edward, uh -- He knows me.
Mr. Thomas: Dennis. Dennis, did you just come off the night shift? Hmm?
Dennis: Yes, sir
Mr. Thomas: Do you know this young lady?
Dennis: She's with Mr. Lewis.
Mr. Thomas: Mr. Lewis?
Vivian: That's it. Edward Lewis! Thanks, Dennis.
Dennis: Evidently she joined him last night.
Mr. Thomas: Thank you.
Vivian: Oh, God. What now? What? What is with everybody today?
Mr. Thomas: No, no. It's all right. Just come with me. We'll have a little chat. Thank you Dennis, thank you. What's your name, miss?
Vivian: What do you want it to be?
Mr. Thomas: Don't play with me, young lady.
Vivian: Vivian.
Mr. Thomas: Thank you Vivian. Well, Miss Vivian... things that go on in other hotels don't happen at the Regent Beverly Wilshire.

(*Vivian says nothing.*)

Mr. Thomas :Now Mr. Lewis, however, is a very special customer, and we like to think of our special customers as friends. Now, as a customer, we would expect Mr. Lewis to sign in any additional guests. But as a friend, we're willing to overlook it. Now I'm assuming you're a... Relative?

Vivian :Yes.

Mr. Thomas : I thought so. You must be his...?

Vivian : Niece?

Mr. Thomas : Of course. Naturally, when Mr. Lewis leaves, I won't see you in this hotel again.

(*Vivian bites her lower lip, nods.*)

Mr. Thomas : I assume you have no other uncles here. Good! Then we understand each other. I would also encourage you... to dress in a more appropriately ; that'll be all.

Vivian : No, that's not all. That's what I was trying to do. I tried to go... get a dress on Rodeo Drive today, and the women wouldn't help me. And I have all this money now and no dress! Not that I expect you to help me, but I have all of this, okay? I have to buy a dress for dinner tonight. And no body will help me... Oh, man, if you're calling in the cops. Yeah, call the cops. That's great. Tell them said hi.

Mr. Thomas : (*into the phone*) Women's clothing. Bridget, please.

Mr. Thomas : Yes, Bridget, hello, this is Barnard Thomas here at the Regent Beverly Wilshire. Thank you, yes, but I'd like to do a favor for me, please. I'm sending someone over. Her name is Vivian. She's a special guest. She's the niece of a very special guest.

Manager : On to new business. Mr. Radcliff is checking out of 709. Mr. Greenwald is checking in. He's back on the wagon, so let's clear out the minibar. Kanga CFO, Mr. Fukimoro, is checking into 814. Stock Evian, shampoo the rugs and extra slippers for his guests. Marisa, heads upon the Madison Suite.

Marisa : Housekeeping.

(*one minute later*)

Manager : Mrs. Sage is arriving with the children... preferably after Mr. Sage's girlfriend departs.

(*one minute later*)

Manager : Let's make sure it's a smooth transition. The Guedj sisters are back. We'll track them on surveillance... but do keep an eye on all bathrobes, cutlery and light fixtures. Sotheby's director, Caroline Lane, has switched from the Four Seasons. She requested a park view...and favors purple orchids and lavender scents. Assemblyman Chris Marshall arrives today. He's gearing up his campaign...so his suite will be doubling as a conference center...with the liquor and coffee bars turning over every four hours. And he's bringing his large dog, so we'll need proper accouterments. And finally, Mr. Newman is back in the Sherman Suite. Careful, ladies, he's a full monty.

(*one minute later*)

Kihoe : I had no idea anyone was here. Don't worry about it, Mr. Monty.

Marisa : No big deal. And I do mean no big deal.

Kihoe & Marisa : No big deal.

(*one minute later*)

Manager : Lavender! You're very creative, Marisa.

Marisa : Thank you, ma'am.

Chapter 4. Dealing with Problems

Unit 1. Emergency First Aid Needed

M: Manager, **G**: Guest

Dialogue 1

G : Ow! ... Help!
M : Let me help you, sir. Are you injured?
G : I think I did something to my ankle.
M : Right. Let's take it easy and don't move too much. Here, let me put this cushion under your head.
(*She is calling the emergency services...*)
G : We have an injured guest at the Hayatt Seoul. Please get a crew here right away.

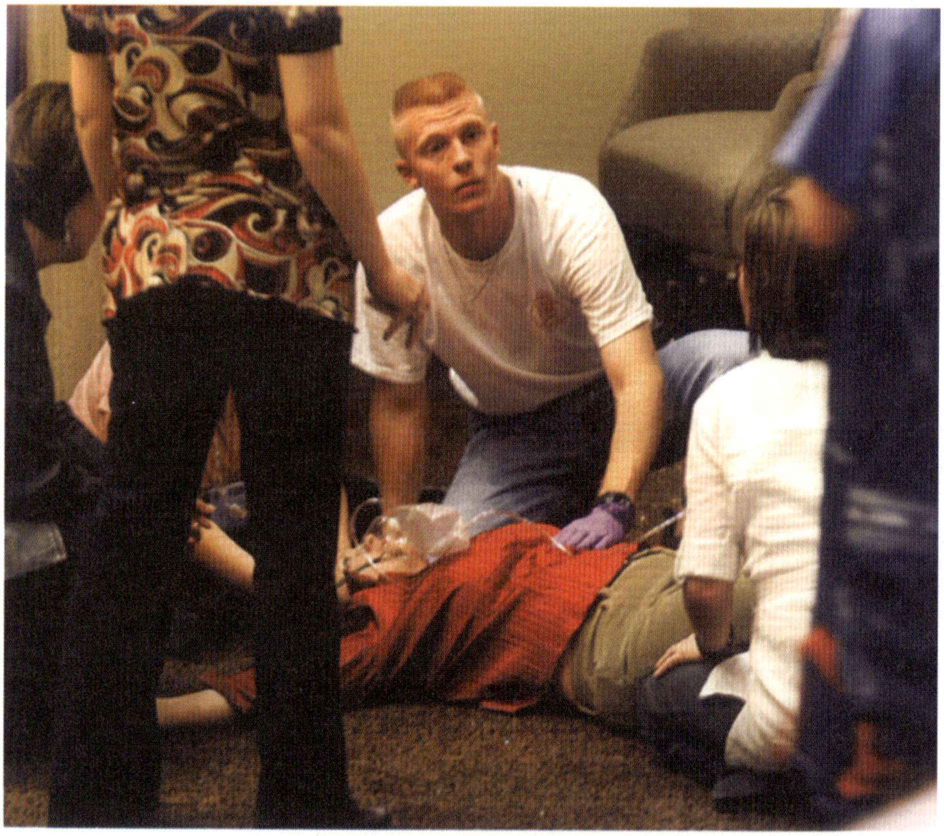

R: Reception, **G**: Guest

Dialogue 2

G : Reception, It's Mrs. Parsons from room 767. My son has just fallen over and cut his head badly at bathroom.
R : Right I'll get the first aid equipment and come straight up. Don't move him. We should call an ambulance. They'll be here soon.
G : Oh, yes... thank you.

Dialogue 3

R: Reception, **G**: Guest

G : My son has a terrible toothache. Can you give me the number of an emergency dentist?

R : Yes, of course. It's 654 9876. There is a pharmacy across the road. I'm sure the pharmacist will give you something for the pain.

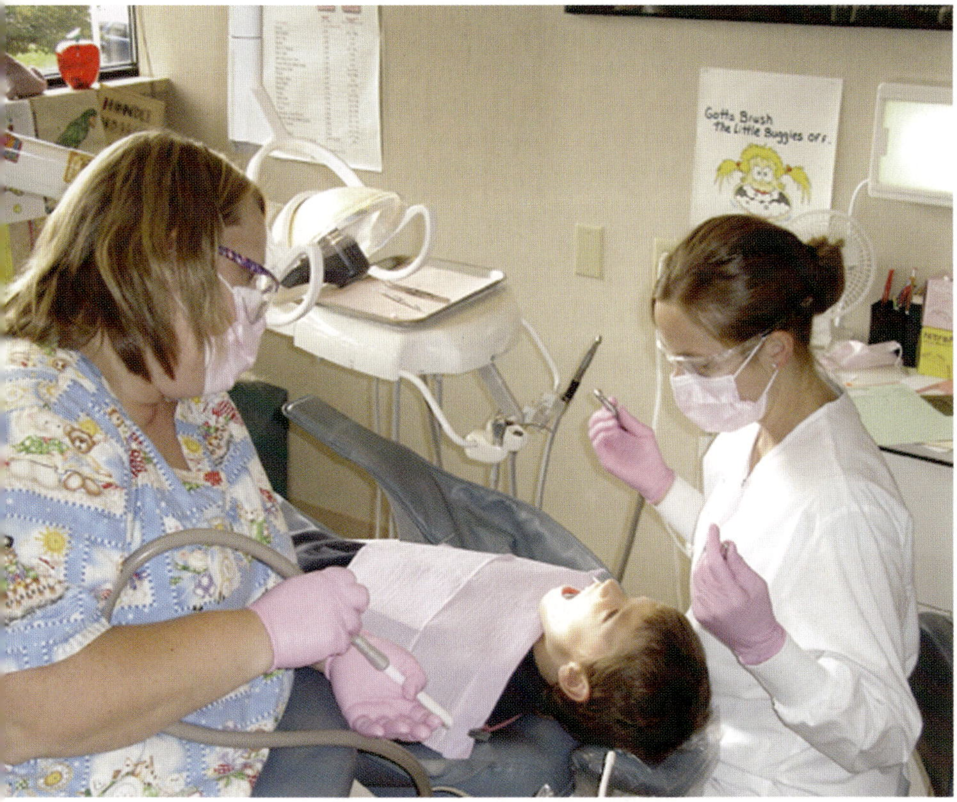

Vocabulary

- fall
- injure
- ankle
- cushion
- crew
- right away
- fall over
- cut his head
- first aid equipment
- ambulance
- terrible
- toothache
- emergency
- dentist
- pharmacy
- pharmacist
- pain

Activities

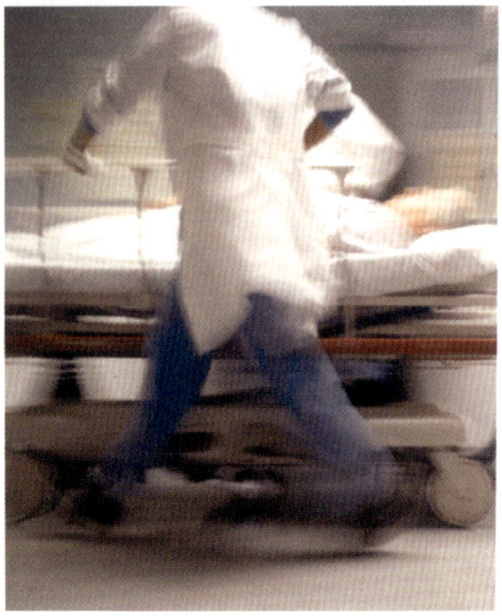

※ *Work with partner. There has been an accident. Discuss the following actions and decide which ones you* ***should do*** *and which you* ***shouldn't do****. Then put them in order of importance.*

A woman has dived into the swimming pool and cut her head badly. She has climbed out and is sitting on the ground.

- ☐ Call an ambulance.
- ☐ Call a lifeguard.
- ☐ Call a first aider.
- ☐ Call a taxi.
- ☐ Give her some food.
- ☐ Massage her head.
- ☐ Cover her in a warm blanket.
- ☐ Fill in an accident report form.
- ☐ Move her.
- ☐ Give her painkiller.
- ☐ Get her a hot drink.
- ☐ Give her cognac.
- ☐ Ask her to lie down.
- ☐ Ask her to walk around.

Unit 2. Dealing with Dissatisfied Guests

Dialogue 1

R: Reception, **G**: Guest

G : Reception, I requested a non-smoking room, but this room really smells of smoke.

R : I'm very sorry. Your request should have been registered. I'll change your room immediately.

Dialogue 2

R: Reception, **G**: Guest

G : I didn't have a wake-up call this morning, but I asked for one for 6.30.

R : Room 234. Yes, you should have had a call. I'm very sorry, I'll look into it.

R: Reception, G: Guest

Dialogue 3

G : Excuse me, but my room hasn't been serviced. The bed hasn't been made and the bathroom hasn't been cleaned.

R : I'm very sorry. It should have been done this morning. I'll call the housekeeper straightaway.

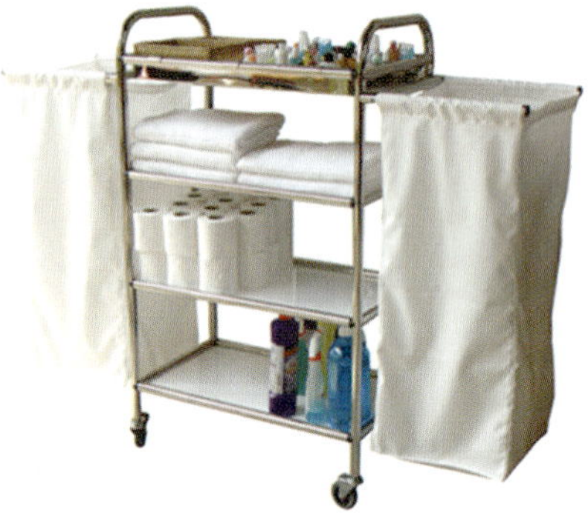

Vocabulary

- request
- smell
- smoke
- register
- wake-up call
- housekeeper

※ *Look at these complaints. What should have been done?*

Example The air conditioning doesn't work. (fix)
It *should have been fixed.*

1. The light bulb is broken. (replace)

2. Our bathroom is dirty. (clean)

3. The rubbish bin is full. (empty)

4. These dishes are dirty. (wash)

5. The satellite TV isn't working. (mend)

※ *What would you say to guests in these situations?*

Example The bed isn't made.
I'm sorry, it *should have been made.*
I'll send someone immediately.

1. Our bath hasn't been mended.

2. The minibar is empty.

3. The bathroom doesn't have any new soap or shampoo.

4. We ordered room service twenty minutes ago.

5. We asked for a quieter room.

■ 영화로 배워보는 Hospitality English (7) - 1408

Woman : Front desk.
Mike : Hello, this is Mike Enslin. Guess which room.
Woman : Good evening, sir.
Mike : Good evening.
Woman : Are you ready to check out?
Mike : Check out? No no no no no. Check out, check out, no. Why would I check out? Especially with this wonderful maid service. It's so discreet. No no no, I need you to send somebody to fix my thermostat. Room's on fire.
Woman : Of course, sir. We'll send an engineer right up.
Mike : You will?
Woman : Absolutely.
Mike : Thank you.
Woman : You're welcome.

Chapter 5. Checking Out

Unit 1. Paying Bills

R: Reception, **G**: Guest

Dialogue 1

G : Hello. We're checking out now. Could we have the bill for room 1235, please? I asked for it to be prepared.

R : Yes, your bill's ready for you, sir. Here you are. Everything is itemized: your room, meals, telephone calls, pay-per-view, and the minibar. Service charge and VAT are included. How would you like to pay?

G : With Visa. Here is my card.

R : Could you sign here, please? Thank you. Here's your receipt and your Visa slip copy. Thank you very much. We hope to see you again.

G : Thank you.

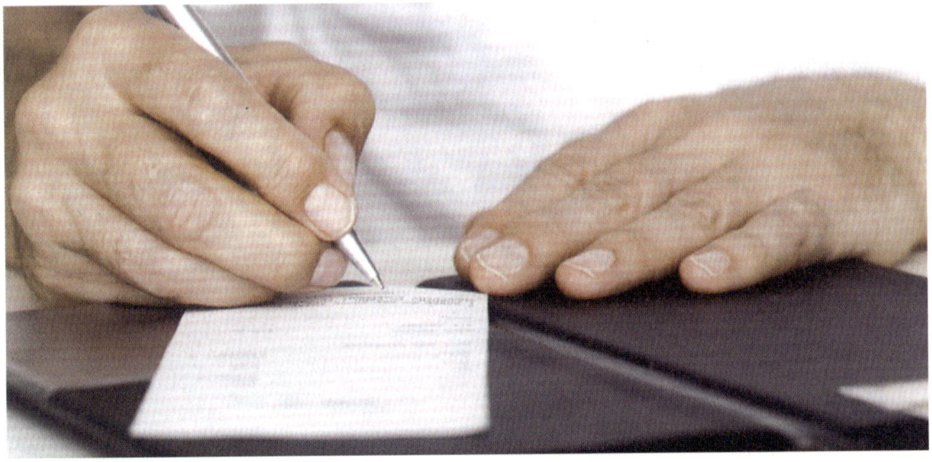

C: Cashier, **G**: Guest

Dialogue 2

C : Your hotel vouchers are for room and breakfast, Mr. Lyons. Your bill for the other meals and drinks comes to 280 dollars. How would you like to pay?

G : With US dollar traveller's checks, please.

Dialogue 3

C : Cashier, G: Guest

G : I'm checking out today. Here are my keys.
C : Yes, sir. Did you enjoy your stay with us?
G : Yes, I did. Thank you.
C : The invoice for your room and meals goes directly to your company.
G : Yes, that's right.
C : So, here's your bill for the extras. How are you paying, sir?
G : With Master card.

Vocabulary

- bill
- itemize
- pay-per-view
- VAT
- slip
- voucher
- come to
- traveller's check
- invoice
- go
- extra

Activities

※ *Look at the examples. And complete these sentences with* ***the correct objective pronoun****.*

Example Could you bring *us* the bill please?
I've included *them* here.

1. A: Where is your luggage?
   B: I gave ________ to the porter.
2. A: Did you tell Mr. Parsons his wife called?
   B: Yes, I gave ________ the message.
3. A: Where is Mrs. Smith?
   B: I saw ________ a moment ago.
4. A: I hope you and your wife enjoyed your stay.
   B: We did, thank you. You looked after ______ very well.
5. A: Goodbye.
   B: Goodbye. We hope to see ________ again soon.

Unit 2. Payment Queries

Dialogue 1

R: Reception, **G**: Guest

G : Hello. I'm in room 1032 and I'd like to settle my bill.

R : 1032. Here we are, sir. Are you paying by American Express?

G : Yes, but just a moment. What are all these items? How much is the minibar bill?

R : Eighty dollars.

G : Eighty dollars! Sue, how many drinks did you have?

R : Oh, just a few... and some snacks.

G : And look at the phone calls! We didn't make many phone calls. This amount is ridiculous.

R : One moment, I'll just check for you. No, you didn't make many calls but there was one very expensive call to Japan on Friday evening.

G : Friday evening? S--u--e--...

Dialogue 2

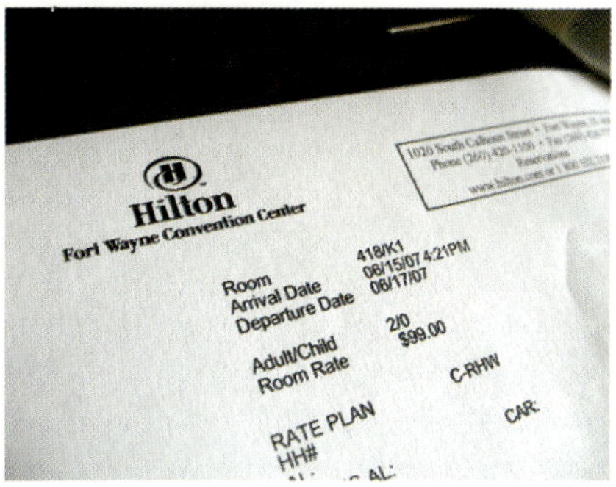

R: Reception, **G**: Guest

G : Could I have a bill please?

R : Thank you, madam.

G : Excuse me, I think there's a mistake. There are a lot of items for room service here but I didn't have much wine or any salads. This looks too much.

R : I'm sorry, madam. This isn't your bill. It's room 1042. One moment, I'll get the right bill for you. Here you are. I'm sorry about that.

G : Ah, that's better. Here is my Visa.

R : Thank you, madam.

Vocabulary

- settle
- pay
- drink
- snack
- make a phone call
- expensive
- mistake

※ *Look the examples and complete the sentences with* ***much****,* ***many*** *or* ***a lot of****. In some cases more than one answer is possible.*

Example I don't have *much* money.
How *many* rooms are booked tonight?

1. There aren't ______________ people tonight.
2. How ______________ single rooms do you have?
3. Is there ______________ work to do this evening?
4. There are ______________ beds to change.
5. We don't have ______________ time.
6. There's ______________ information on our web site.
7. How ______________ money do you have?

PartⅡ. In the Restaurants

Chapter 6. Reservations

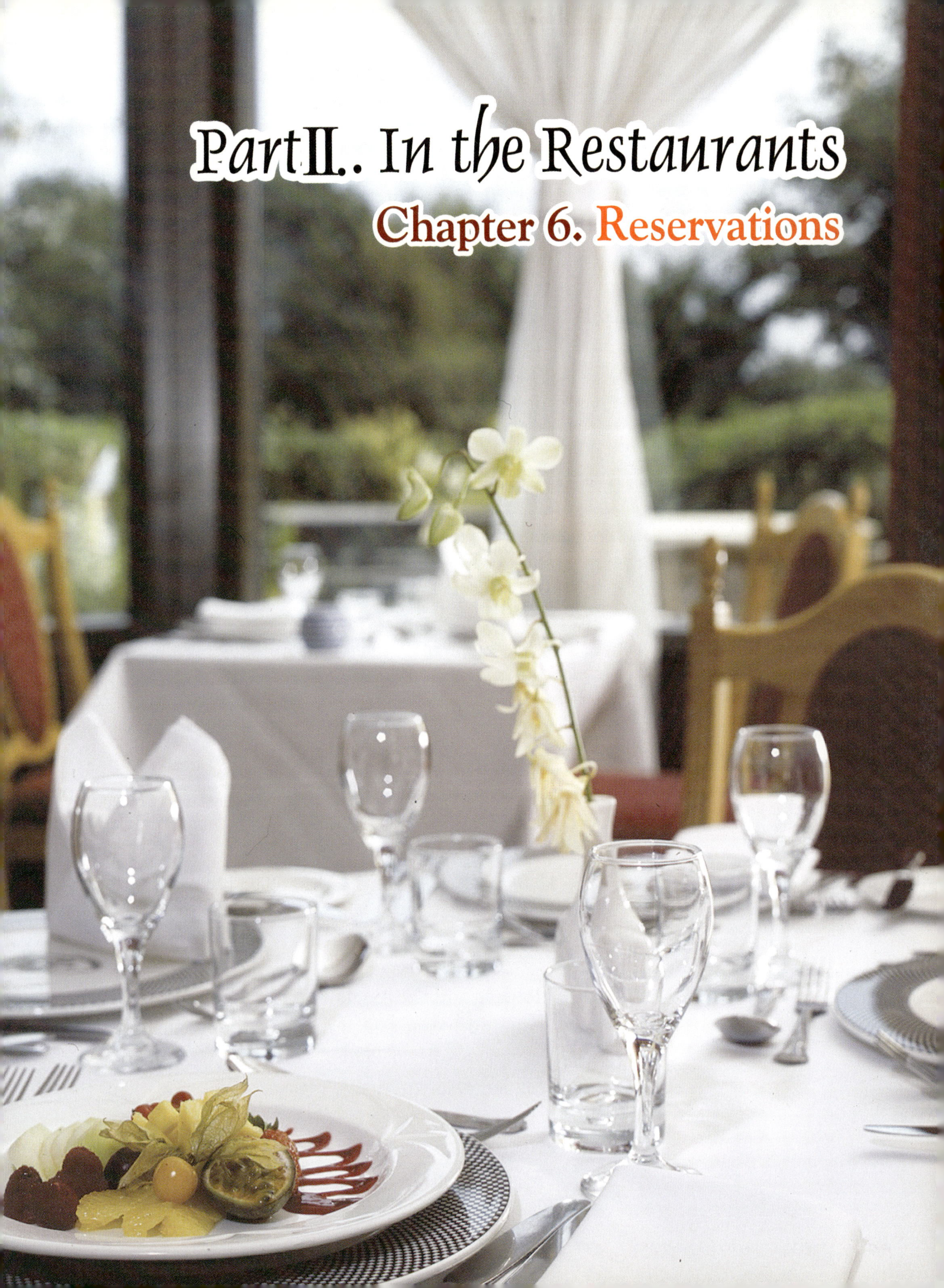

Unit 1. Taking a Restaurant Reservation

M: Manager, C: Customer

Dialogue 1

C : Good morning, I'd like to book a table, please. What days do you open?

M : We open from Tuesday to Sunday. And we close on Mondays.

C : I see. What time do you serve dinner?

M : We serve dinner from seven o'clock to 11 pm.

C : O.K. I'd like to book a table for six people at eight o'clock on Saturday on the 13th of August, please.

M : We're always busy on Saturdays. We sometimes have cancellations but I'm afraid we're fully booked on Saturday on the 13th of August. Oh... but we have a table on the 12th.

C : OK. Friday on the 12th is fine. Thank you.

M : So...That's a table for six at 7 pm on Friday on the 12th of August.

C : Yes, please.

M : What name is it, please?

C : Vivian... V-I-V-I-A-N.

M : OK. We look forward to seeing you on Friday on the 12th of August.

M: Manager, C: Customer

Dialogue 2

M : Good afternoon, Ratatouille restaurant. Can I help you?

C : Hello. I'd like to make a reservation. Can I have a table for two at 7:30 on Thursday evening?

M : Yes, sir. And your name please?

C : Mr. Gerard Butler.

M : Do you have a contact number?

C : Yes, my mobile number is 06780132456.

M : Thank you, Mr. Butler.

M: Manager, C: Customer

Dialogue 3

M : Good afternoon. The Olive restaurant. How may I help you?

C : Yes. Hello. My name is Mark Levin. I'd like to make a reservation for lunch tomorrow. There are 4 of us, and we'd like a table about 1:30 pm.

M : Hold on a second, I'll check it... Yes, Mr. Levin. We have some very nice window tables for four at 1:30 pm.

C : Lovely.

M : And would you like smoking or non-smoking?

C : Non-smoking area, please. And it's my wife's birthday. Could you put a bouquet of a dozen red roses on the table?

M : Certainly, Mr. Levin. We'll just add that to your bill.

C : OK. Thanks.

M : We'll see you at 1:30 pm tomorrow afternoon, Mr. Levin. The roses will be on the table before you're seated.

C : Thank you very much. Bye.

Vocabulary

- serve
- cancellation
- have a table
- contact number
- hold on a second
- window table
- bouquet
- seat

Activities

※ *Read the notes and make questions and answers.*

Example what / the restaurant serve dinner (7:00 - 10:30)
What time does the restaurant serve dinner?
From 7:00 to 10:30.

1. when / the restaurant open for lunch (12:15 - 3:00 p.m.)

2. what / my flight leave (18:20)

3. when / the group arrive from England (6:45 p.m.)

4. when / the cafe close (11:30 p.m.)

5. what / the exchange bureau open (8:00 a.m.)

Activities

※ *Read the notes and make questions and answers.*

Example

What time is it?

- It's one fifteen.
- It's a quarter past one.

1.

2.

3.

4.

Unit 2. Explaining That No Table Is Available

M: Manager, C: Customer

Dialogue 1

M : Do you have reservations?

C : No.

M : Hmmm. I'm afraid we're very full at the moment. There will be at least an hour's wait.

C : Alex, we need to eat sooner than that.

M : Maybe I can help you find another restaurant near here. Just a moment, please....

(*She rings to a nearby Italian restaurant.*)

M : May I reserve a table, please?

R : Reception, C: Customer

Dialogue 2

C : I'd like to book a table for Tuesday lunch.

R : I'm sorry, ma'am. We only open in the evenings.

Dialogue 3

M: Manager, C: Customer

M : Marco Polo, Jessie speaking.
C : Oh, hello. Do you have a table for a party of five for tonight?
M : At what time?
C : Eight thirty.
M : We're pretty busy tonight. We have only a table for seven o'clock but not for eight thirty.
C : Hmm... seven is fine.
M : Smoking or no-smoking?
C : Smoking, please.
M : OK. Party of five for seven o'clock. May I have your name, please?
C : Jason Bateman. B-A-T-E-M-A-N.
M : Fine. We'll see you tonight, Mr. Bateman.

Vocabulary

- at least
- wait
- sooner
- nearby
- pretty

Activities

※ *Refuse these requests. Give polite explanations and use the short forms.*

Example Can I reserve a table for tomorrow night?
(no tables)
I'm sorry, we don't have any tables.

1. Can I reserve a table for two for Monday?
(Close on Mondays)

____

2. I'd like to book a family room for the Easter weekend.
(Fully booked)

____

3. Can I have a parking space, please?
(full)

____

4. I'd like to speak to Mr. Jeong in room 762, please.
(no answer)

____

5. I'd like to book a table for Sunday lunch.
(only open evenings)

____

Chapter 7. Ordering

Unit 1. Taking an Order(1)

W : Waiter, G1: Guest1, G2 : Guest2

Dialogue 1

W : Good evening, sir. A table for two?

G1 : Yes, please. The name's Bulter.

W : I'll show you to your table. This way. Can I take your coats?

G1 : Thank you.

W : Here's the menu and wine list. Can I get you an aperitif?

G1 : Yes, please. A gin and tonic.

G2 : And the same for me.

W : Thank you.

S: Server, G: Guest

Dialogue 2

S : My name is Lisa. I'll be your server today. Can I get you something to drink?

G : Yes, I'd like whatever light beer you have, and my wife will have some orange juice on the rocks. And some water, please.

S : I have the water right here. I'll just go and place your order while you look at the menu.

Dialogue 3

W: Waitress, G1: Guest1, G2: Guest2

W : Are your ready to order now?
G1 : Yes, I think so. What' the soup of the day?
W : It's mushroom and potatoes.
G1 : I think I'll have the avocado and prawn tart to start with, followed by the salmon.
G2 : And the goat's cheese salad for me please, followed by the fillet steak.
W : How would you like the steak cooked?
G2 : Medium rare, please.
W : And would you like to order some wine?
G1 : Yes, what about the Cabernet Sauvignon, Sue?
G2 : I think I'd prefer white. Why don't you have half a bottle of the Cabernet and I'll have a glass of Chablis. And can we have a bottle of mineral water please?
W : Still or sparkling?
G2 : Still, please.
W : OK. Coming right up.

Vocabulary

- show
- menu
- wine list
- aperitif
- gin and tonic
- server
- on the rocks
- place an order
- soup
- mushroom
- still
- avocado
- prawn
- tart
- salmon
- fillet steak
- medium
- rare
- Cabernet Sauvignon
- Chablis
- mineral water
- sparkling

Activities

※ *Complete the sentences with* ***a/an*** *or* ***some***.

Example I'd like *a* bottle of red wine
I'd like *some* bread.

1. Would you like ________ milk?
2. Could we have ________ water?
3. Can I have ________ ice in my orange juice?
4. Just ________ glass of white wine, please.
5. Would you like ________ aperitif ?

※ *Read the situation of the example. What questions would you ask customers in the situation? Some questions have been provided for you. Try to add more.*

Example

■ **Situation**: You work at the front desk in a hotel.
A customer comes in and says he/she wants a room for two nights.

■ **Possible questions**.

For how many people?
Do you want a room with a view?
Smoking or non-smoking?

1. ■ **Situation** : You are a food server in a restaurant.
A customer asks for a salad and a soft drink.

■ **Possible questions**.

____

____

____

2. ■ **Situation** : You are a manager of an Italian restaurant.
A guest comes in and says he/she wants to book a table for tomorrow.

■ **Possible questions**.

____

____

____

Unit 2. Taking an Order(2)

Dialogue 1

W : Waiter, G1 : Guest 1 G2 : Guest 2

W : What would you like for breakfast, madam?

G1 : Coffee with full milk and croissant, please.

G2 : I'll have egg and bacon, and a pot of tea. And some toast, please.

W : Thank you, sir. Can I have your room number?

Dialogue 2

W: Waiter, G1: Guest 1, G2: Guest 2

W : Are you ready to order, sir?

G1 : I just want a light lunch. I'll have basil and tomato soup and a toasted sandwich. Cheese and ham, please.

W : And for you, little lady?

G2: Hmm... the chef's salad and a piece of cheese pizza, please. And fanta lemon flavor.

W : OK. I'll be in a moment.

W: Waiter, G1: Guest1, G2: Guest2

Dialogue 3

W : I'll get these out of your way. Here are some dessert menus.
G1 : Not for me, thanks. I'm full!
G2 : That cheesecake sounds really lovely.
W : Would you like some coffee?
G2 : No, thanks.
G1 : Sure. Decaf, please.

Vocabulary

- full milk
- croissant
- pot
- basil
- toast
- sandwich
- flavor
- get out of
- dessert
- menu
- sound
- decaf.(=*decaffeinated*)

※ *Complete the sentences with* ***some*** *or* ***any****.*

1. Do you have __________ fresh fruit?

2. Could we have __________ water, please?

3. Would you like __________ coffee?

4. Can I get you __________ more drinks?

5. There isn't __________ cheese.

※ *Make questions and answers.*

Example apple tart (cream or ice cream)

A: Can I have some apple tart, please?

B: Would you like it with cream or ice cream?

A: Ice cream, please.

1. coffee (milk or without milk)

2. steak (sweet potatoes or fried rice)

3. salad (French dressing or Island dressing)

Unit 3. About Menu

W : Waiter, G: Guest

Dialogue 1

G : Excuse me, could you please explain the menu to us?

W: Yes, of course.

G : What's in the penne arrabbiata?

W: Well, this is a pasta dish. It consists of penne, a type of pasta, in a chilli and tomato sauce. It's made from chilli, tomato, garlic and basil.

G : Sounds good. I'll take it.

W: Waiter, G: Guest

Dialogue 2

W: Are you ready to order? For you, madam?

G : Well, could you explain this seafood dish?

W: This is a dish for two people. It contains half a lobster, king prawns, scallops, and mussels. And it's served warm with a crisp, green salad.

G : Hmm...sounds lovely.

W: Waiter, G: Guest

Dialogue 3

W: How was your steak with garlic sauce?

G: That was very nice, thank you.

W: Good, I'm very glad you enjoyed it. Would you like the dessert menu?

G: Yes, please. Do you have any ice cream?

W: Yes, we do. There's vanilla, chocolate, and there's also blackcurrant sorbet. Here's the menus. We also have a special board. Today we have a pumpkin pie, French apple tart, and hazelnut meringue with summer berries.

G: Oh, I'll have the blackcurrant sorbet, please.

Vocabulary

- dish
- consist of
- sauce
- made from
- garlic
- basil
- lobster
- king prawn
- scallops
- mussels
- crisp
- special board
- sorbet
- pudding
- meringue

Activities

※ *Change these sentences to the* ***Passive*** *form.*

1. We make pasta from flour, eggs and salt.

2. You make a Margarita with tequila.

3. The receptionist tells guests about the hotel facilities.

4. The restaurant serves dinner from 6.00 to 11.00.

5. We make dressing from oil and vinegar.

※ *Make sentences using the correct* ***Passive*** *form.*

Example The table *is laid* in the evening.

1. table	lay	in the evening
2. tablecloth	place	on the table
3. napkin	fold and place	on the side plate
4. knife and fork	place	each side of the plate
5. wine glass	put	above the soup spoon
6. salt and pepper	put	in the middle of the table
7. main course plate	take away	when the main course is finished
8. dessert spoon and fork	bring	with the dessert menu
9. flower arrangement	place	next to the salt and pepper

영화로 배워보는 Hospitality English (8) - Ratatouille

Waiter: Do you know what you would like this evening, sir?

Ego : Yes, I think I do. After reading a lot of overheated puffery about your new cook, you know what I'm craving? A little perspective. That's it. I'd like some fresh, clear, well seasoned perspective. Can you suggest a good wine to go with that?

Waiter: With what, sir?

Ego : Perspective. Fresh out, I take it?

Waiter: I am...

Ego : Very well. Since you're all out of perspective and no one else seems to have it in this bloody town, I'll make you a deal. You provide the food, I'll provide the perspective. Which would go nicely with a bottle of Cheval Blanc 1947.

Waiter: I'm afraid. Ummm... Your dinner selection?

Ego : Tell your Chef Linguini that I want whatever he dares to serve me. Tell him to hit me with his best shot.

Various Glasses in Restaurant

• Champagne Glasses

• Red Wine Glasses

• White Wine Glasses

• Rose Wine Glasses

• Port / Sherry Wine Glasses

• Spirits Glasses

• Brown Spirits Glasses

• Basic Glasses

Chapter 8. Payment

Unit 1. Taking a Payment

C: Cashier, G: Guest

Dialogue 1

C : How was your dinner, madam?
G : It was delicious. Thank you.
C : I'm glad you enjoyed it with us. How would you like to pay?
G : I'll pay in cash.
C : Here is your change. Thank you.

W: Waiter, G: Guest

Dialogue 2

G : Excuse me, We're leaving now. Could you bring us the bill, please?
W : Certainly, sir.
G : Have you included the drinks from the bar?
W : Yes, I've included them here. How are you paying?
G : I'm paying in cash. Do you accept Euros?
W : Yes, we do. The total in Euros is just there. Would you like a VAT receipt?
G : No, thanks. This is fine.

S: Server, G: Guest

Dialogue 3

S : Could I bring you anything else?
G : No, thank you. We have to leave.
S : Could I bring you the bill?
G : Yes, please. We're the guests at the hotel.
S : Should I just charge it to your room?
G : Yes, please.
S : What's your room number?
G : Room 4321.
S : 4321. OK, sign here please.

Vocabulary

- delicious
- pay
- change
- bring
- bill
- include
- receipt
- charge

Activities

※ *Complete the sentences with the **Present Perfect** of the verbs in brackets. Use short forms if appropriate.*

Example I'*ve* just *spoken* (speak) to Mr. Smith on the phone.

1. We ____________ (not have) lunch yet.
2. I ____________ (write) the manager a letter. Here it is.
3. They ____________ (not see) the new Spanish restaurant yet.
4. Hanna ________ just ____________ (go) to the office.
5. The sommelier ____________ (not take) his order yet.

※ *Complete the sentences with the **Present Perfect** or **Past Simple** of the verbs in brackets. Use short forms if appropriate.*

Example **A** : *Have* you *whisked* (whisk) the cream yet?
B : Yes, I whisked (whisk) it after I chopped the apple.

1. **A** : ________ the Korean group ____________ (check in) yet?
   B : They ________ (arrive) about an hour ago. They ________ (be) in their rooms for half an hour.

2. **A** : ________ Mr and Mrs Parsons ________ (come) back yet?
   B : No, they ________ (not). They ________ (say) they would be back late.

Unit 2. Credit Card Problems

Dialogue 1

C: Cashier, G: Guest

C : Is everything all right?
G : Yes, excellent. Thank you.
C : How would you like to pay?
G : With Mastercard.
(*A cashier swiped the credit card through the card reader, however the machine rejected the card.*)
C : I'm sorry, sir. This card is not working for some reason.
G : Oh, my mistake. This one has expired. Let's try another one.
C : Sure.
(*The machine accepted the new card.*)
C : Could you sign here, please? Thank you.

Dialogue 2

C: Cashier, G: Guest

C : How are you paying for this?
G : With American Express. Here's my card.
C : I'm sorry. We only accept Visas or Master Cards, ma'am.
G : I see. Here's a visa.

Dialogue 3

C : Did you enjoy the lunch?

G : Yes, we did. The service was wonderful.

C : That comes to 110,000 won. How would you like to pay, sir?

G : I'll put it on my Visa.

(*The cashier swiped the credit card but the transaction failed.*)

C : I'm sorry, sir. This card is not working for some reason. Might be a problem with the magnetic strip.

G : Umm... Can you try this one, with MasterCard?

C : Sure, thank you.

Vocabulary

- excellent
- swipe
- card reader
- machine
- reject
- work
- mistake
- accept
- come to
- transaction
- magnetic strip

Activities

※ *Compete the dialogue between 2 guests using **did/didn't**.*

A : ________ you check in OK this morning?

B : Yes, I ________. ________ you have to fill in a registration cad?

A : Yes, I ________ Actually, my wife filled it in.

B : ________ she leave your passport at reception?

A : No, she ________. The receptionist took the numbers and gave them back.

________ you get your passport back?

B : No, I ________. I must remember to pick it up.

Sample Menu for Activity

Full Course Dinner

1. Palate cleanser, or amuse
2. Second amuse
3. Caviar
4. Cold appetizer
5. Thick soup
6. Thin soup
7. Shellfish
8. Antipasto
9. Pasta
10. Intermezzo (Sorbet)
11. Quail
12. Wild mushrooms
13. Beef
14. Green salad
15. Pudding
16. Ice cream
17. Puffed pastry filled with herbed mousse
18. Cheese
19. Fruit
20. Coffee
21. Petit four

※**a la carte** - a menu having individual dishes listed with separate prices ; (*of a restaurant meal*) having unlimited choices with a separate price for each item

bolla
modern italian

Welcomes

KRLD RESTAURANT WEEK

August 11-24, 2008

Starter

Arugula Insalata. House Ricotta. Sicilian Olive Oil. Cracked Pepper

or

Heirloom Tomato Salad . Buffala Mozzarella . Basil Seeds

Wine Pairing

San Giuseppe . Pinot Grigio . Veneto

Entrée

Skate Wing . Tomato Risotto . Crisp Asparagus . Parmesan Broth

or

Charred Beef Tenderloin . Truffle-Onion Crumble . Parmesan Potatoes . Buerre Rouge

Wine Pairing

Michele Chiarlo . Barbera d'Asti . Piedmont

Optional Central Market Fourth Course

Risotto Primavera . Chef's Daily Inspiration

Dessert

Carnaroli Rice Pudding . Pistachio Custard . Caramel Bon Bons

or

Semi Freddo. Chocolate Amaretti. Blackberries

THREE COURSES $35

WITH ABOVE WINE PAIRING $45

CENTRAL MARKET RISOTTO PRIMAVERA COURSE: $10

CHEF DAVID BULL

Chapter 9.
Dealing with Problems

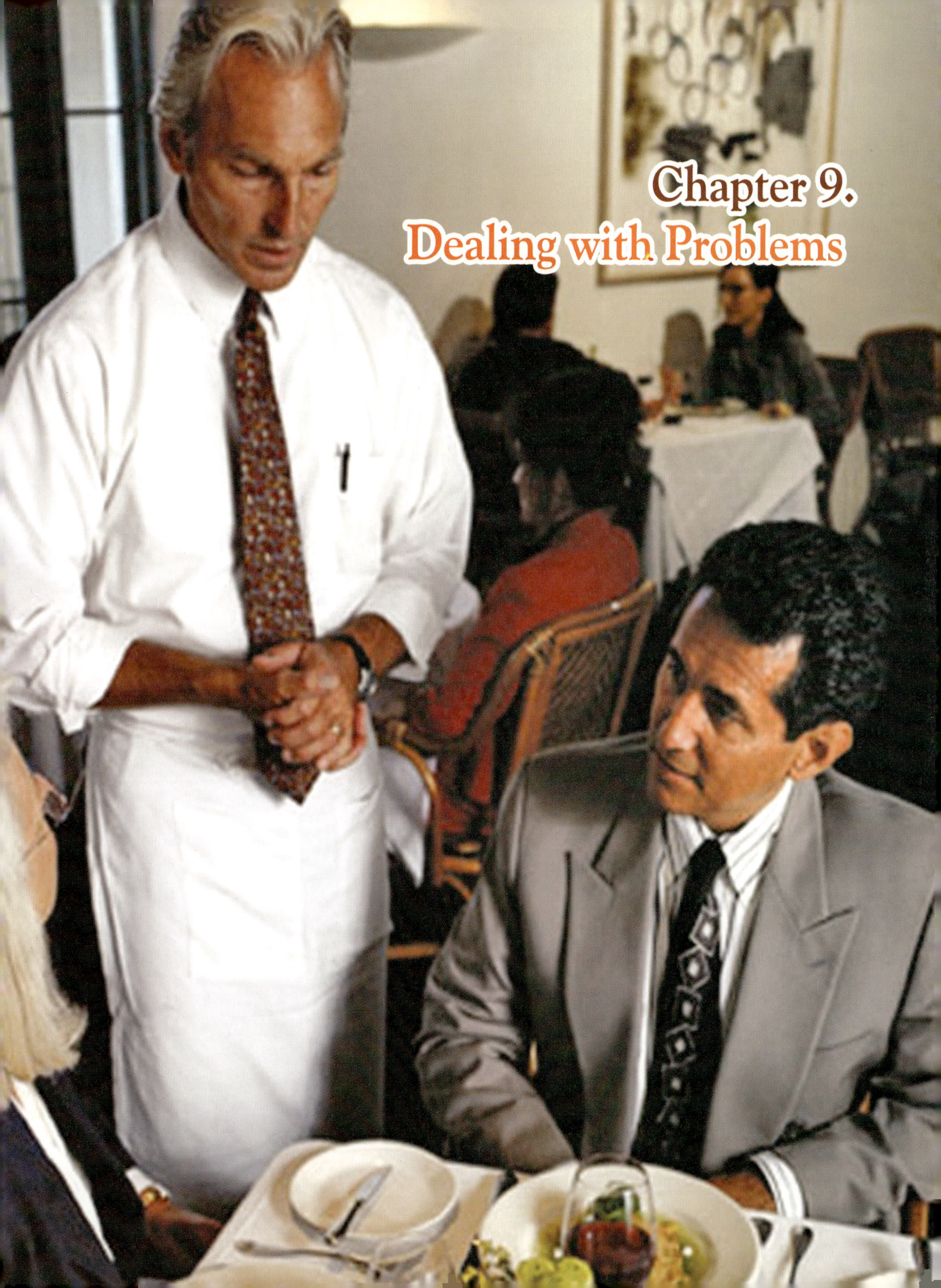

Unit 1. Dealing with Problems(1)

W : Waiter,   G: Guest

Dialogue 1

G : Excuse me, I wanted my steak well-done, but it's very rare.
W: I'm sorry about that. I'll send it back to the kitchen.
G : Thanks. One more thing. This fork is dirty.
W: I'm so sorry. I'll get you a clean one.

M: Manager,   G: Guest

Dialogue 2

G : Excuse me, my fish was undercooked. And my daughter's chicken was dry and overcooked.
M: I'm very sorry, ma'am. I'll speak to the chef and bring you both new ones.
G : No, thanks. We have to hurry this afternoon.
M: I deeply apologize for what happened.
G : It's alright. Please be more careful next time.
M: Of course. Your meal is on the house.
G : Great! Does that include dessert, too?
M: Sure!

W: Waiter, G: Guest

Dialogue 3

G : Excuse me, we ordered our dishes 40 minutes ago.

W : I'm very sorry, sir. I'll be with you in a moment. The restaurant is short-staffed tonight. I'll check with your food at the kitchen right now.

Vocabulary

- undercook
- overcook
- apologize
- on the house
- include
- short-staffed

Activities

※ *Complete the sentences with the* ***Present Simple*** *active or* ***Passive*** *of the verbs in brackets.*

1. We ______ (open) the restaurant every day at 12.00.
2. The rooms ______ (clean) every morning.
3. First, you ______ (chop) the onions.
4. Ice Vine ______ (produce) in Germany.
5. The dish ______ (not serve) cool. It ______ (serve) cold.

Unit 2. Dealing with Problems (2)

W: Waiter, G: Guest

Dialogue 1

G : Could I have a bill, please?
W : Certainly, sir.
G : Excuse me, I think there is a mistake. What is this charge for? We didn't order this menu.
W : I'm sorry, sir. This isn't your bill. It's table fourteen's. Just a moment, please. I'll get the right bill for you... Here we are. I'm very sorry about that.
G : Ah, that's better. Here's my Visa card.
W : Thank you, sir...

W: Waiter, G: Guest

Dialogue 2

G : Excuse me, this beer's flat.
W : I'm sorry, sir. I'll get you another.

W: Waiter,   G: Guest

Dialogue 3

G : Excuse me, this table is too small. There are eight of us.
W : I'm sorry, sir. I'll change your table straightaway.
G : And one more thing, this glass is cracked.
W : I'm terribly sorry, sir. I'll get you anther one.

Vocabulary

- charge
- flat
- crack

※ *Complete the sentences with* ***much, many*** *or* ***a lot of***.

1. There aren't __________ people in the restaurant.
2. How __________ twin rooms do you have?
3. We don't have __________ time.
4. How __________ drinks did you have?
5. We didn't have __________ wine.
6. How __________ tables are booked tonight?
7. I don't have __________ money.

Guest : My wife's foie gras hasn't been cooked long enough.

Chef : Excuse me?

Manager : Why don't I bring you... a new appetizer with my compliments?

Chef : My foie gras is perfectly cooked.

Guest : Nothing to be ashamed of, honey. Even the best stumble over foie gras.

Chef : There's nothing wrong with this. It's perfectly comme il faut.

Guest : What is that supposed to mean?

Chef : Comme il faut? "As it should be." 140 degrees in the oven, 80 degrees water temperature, for 25 minutes...not too long, not too short, with the perfect touch of pink, honey.

Guest : That's it. We'll take our business somewhere else. Let's go.

Chef : May I suggest Vinnie's hot dog stand at the corner? He cooks to order.

Manager : How many times have I told you? You can't make a scene every time someone doesn't like your food.

Chef : Please. The guy is a barbarian.

Manager : And a paying customer. If he says the foie gras is not done, it's not.

Chapter 10. Instructions

Unit 1. Explain How to Do Things

S: Server, T: Trainee

Dialogue 1

T : How do you make a Manhattan?
S : First, half fill a large glass with ice.
T : I see. What next?
S : Next, add one and a half measures of Canadian whisky and three quarters of a measures of sweet vermouth.
T : OK.
S : Then add a dash of Angostura bitters.
T : OK.
S : Then stir it well and strain into cocktail glass.
T : All right.
S : Finally, garnish with a cherry and serve!

I: Instructor, T: Trainee

Dialogue 2

I : This morning I'd like to check you all know the standard restaurant place setting. So Mike, can you start first, please?
T : Yes, first place a clean tablecloth and napkin on the table, and the napkin is correctly folded and placed on the show plate. Then put the butter knife on top of the side plate. Place a main course knife and fork to the right and left of the plate position, and then a fish knife and fork outside them.
I : Good, what else?
T : Finally, put a wine glass above the soup spoon.
I : Good. And don't forget the salt and pepper, a flower arrangement, and if it's the evening, a candle.
T : Yes, sir.

Dialogue 3

T1 : Trainer, T2 : Trainee

T1 : At reception, always welcome customers with a warm smile. Be polite and friendly at all the time.

T2 : Yes, of course.

T2 : What do you do when people make a telephone reservation?

T1 : Always answer the call within three rings or apologize for the delay when you answer. When you know the customer's name, use it in conversation.

T2 : OK. I see.

Vocabulary

- Manhattan
- half
- fill
- bitter
- dash
- stir
- strain
- garnish
- serve
- standard
- measure
- quarter
- vermouth
- table cloth
- napkin
- show plate
- position
- arrangement
- apologize
- delay

Activities

※ *Match each definition with the job.*

1. Someone has to welcome guests and complete the registration form. •	• chef
2. Someone has to make sure that everything in the guests'room is in order. •	• pastry cook
3. Someone should plan the cooking times for dinner. •	• waiter/waitress
4. Someone has to prepare a special cake for the function. •	• receptionist
5. Someone has to take an order from guests and serve dishes to the guests. •	• house keeper

Unit 2. In the Kitchen

C : Chef, T: Trainee

Dialogue 1

C : Right. Today we have to prepare the brunch vegetables, so I'll show you what to do. First, you must wash your hands over there in the hand basin. Let's start with the potatoes. Peel them like this.

T : Is this OK?

C : Good. Then we have to julienne the potatoes. Cut them into little sticks, like this. I'll do that. You sort and wash the onions. Slice the big ones in half.

T : Do we have to chop them?

C : Right. I'll chop the onions and you can do the broccoli. You have to break it into florets and wash it well in cold water. And it mustn't cook for long, only four or five minutes. Then strain it into a colander.

T : OK, I'll start...

C: Chef, T: Trainee

Dialogue 2

C : This morning I'd like to say about kitchen hygiene. Remember that all kitchen staff mustn't wash your hands in the food preparation sinks but always wash their hands in the hand basin.

T : Yes.

C : And you must clean all kitchen work surfaces regularly, and wash and dry all the utensils after use. It's very important the kitchen is clean.

T : OK. How about the rubbish?

C : Yes, for the rubbish the kitchen porters are responsible and they have to clean the bins regularly. The chefs don't have to do this, but they must put the rubbish in the correct bins.

M: Manager, **T**: Trainee

Dialogue 3

M : These are the kitchens. Kate's our head chef. She writes the menus and she is responsible for the main courses. Hello, Bob is the sous-chef and that's his station over there. He prepares all the soups, hot appetizers, and the side orders.

T : Oh, he sounds like busy.

M : Yes, but two commis chefs are responsible to the sous chef, so they help him. And the pastry chef works over there. She bakes all the bread. She prepares the hot desserts.

Vocabulary

- brunch
- hand basin
- peel
- julienne
- sort
- strain
- colander
- kitchen hygiene
- sink
- utensil
- kitchen porter
- appetizer (=*starter*)
- slice
- chop
- broccoli
- florets
- bin
- rubbish
- head chef
- sous chef
- station
- commis chef
- side order

※ *Complete the sentences using* ***must, have to, don't have to, mustn't.***

Activities

1. You ________ have clean hands in the kichen.
2. We ________ start work at 7:30 am.
3. I ________ (not) work on Sundays.
4. We ________ prepare the vegetables before 10.
5. GUests ________ check out by 12 noon.

※ *Match each vegetable with the correct pictures.*

asparagus	cucumber	onion	radish
cabbage	lettuce	pepper	sweetcorn
cauliflower	mushrooms	pumpkin	tomato

※ *Match each utensil with the correct pictures.*

chopping board	peeler	mortar and pestle
dredger	rolling pin	sieve
grater	scissors	skimmer
ladle	mixing bowl	whisk

■ 영화로 배워보는 Hospitality English (10) - Ratatouille

Remy : I can't believe it. A real gourmet kitchen, and I get to watch.

Gusteau : You've read my book. Let us see how much you know, huh? Which one is the chef ?

Remy : Oh, that guy.

Gusteau : Very good. Who is next in command?

Remy : The sous chef. There. The sous is responsible for the kitchen when the chef's not around. Saucier, in charge of sauces. Very important. Chef de partie, demi chef de partie, both important. Commis, commis, they're cooks. Very important.

Gusteau : You are a clever rat. Now, who is that?

Remy : Oh, him? He's nobody.

Not nobody. He is part of the kitchen.

Remy : No, he's a plongeur or something. He washes dishes or takes out the garbage. He doesn't cook.

Appendix

1. Vocabulary Lists
2. Terms of Hotel & Restaurant

Appendix. 1 **Vocabulary Lists**

A

- a bottle of 한 병
- a pair of (두 개로 된) 한 쌍, (두 부분으로 되어 분리할 수 없는) 한 벌
- a single(double, twin, suite) room 1인실(2인용, 특실)
- a single(twin, double) bed 1인용 침대
- accept 받아들이다
- access 인터넷 장치
- accommodation 숙박(수용)설비
- adjoin room 어조이닝 룸
- afraid 유감이지만
- air conditioning 공기조절(장치)
- ambulance 구급차
- ankle 발목
- aperitif 아프리티프 ; 식전주
- apologize 사과하다, 사죄하다
- arrange 준비하다
- at least 적어도
- audio-visual 시청각
- authority 발행기관
- available 이용할 수 있는
- avocado (열대 아메리카산의) 아보카도

B

- B&B(= *Bed&Breakfast*) 조식이 포함된 숙박
- baby sitter 베이비 시터
- banquet 연회
- basement 지하층
- basic 기본적인 것
- basil 허브(향신료의 일종)
- bath 목욕
- bathroom 욕실
- behind 뒤에
- beverage 음료
- bill 계산서
- blanket 담요
- boardroom 회의실
- book(= *reserve*) 예약하다
- book a table 좌석을 예약하다
- bouquet 부케, 꽃다발
- bring 가져오다
- broadband 광역망
- business traveller 상용 여행객

C

- Cabernet Sauvignon 까베르네 쇼비뇽(프랑스 레드와인)
- cancellation 취소
- car hire 차량 대여
- car license plate 차량 번호판
- car registration no.(number) 자동차 등록번호
- card reader 카드판독기
- Chablis 샤블리(프랑스 화이트 와인)
- champagne 샴페인
- change 바꾸다
- charge 요금, 금액, 비용
- check in 체크인, 투숙절차
- city or town 시/도 명
- closet 벽장
- coffee maker 커피메이커
- complimentary 무료의
- concierge 컨시어지
- conference 회의
- confirm 확인하다
- confirmation 확인
- contact 접촉, 연락(을 취함)
- contact number 연락번호
- continental breakfast 유럽식 조찬
- corridor 복도
- crack 깨어지다, 금이 가다
- credit card 신용카드
- crew 구급요원
- crisp 얇게 썬 감자 프라이, 포테이토 칩
- croissant 크루아상, 초승달 모양의 롤 빵
- cushion 쿠션

D

- date of arrival 도착일
- date of birth 출생일
- date of departure 출발일
- date of expire 만료기간
- date of issue 발급일
- decaf.(= *decaffeinated*) 카페인을 제거한 커피
- delicious 맛좋은, 맛있는
- dentist 치과의사
- dessert 디저트, 후식
- dish 큰 접시, 요리
- downtown 도심지
- drapes(= *curtains*) 커튼
- drink 음료
- dry cleaning 드라이클리닝

E

- emergency 비상사태, 비상시, 위급
- equip 갖추어 주다
- equipment 장비, 비품, 설비
- excellent 아주 훌륭한
- exchange bureau 환전소
- expensive 값비싼
- expire 만기가 되다
- extra 여분의

F

- facility 설비, 시설
- fall 떨어지다
- fall over 넘어지다, 엎어지다
- family name(= *surname, last name*) 성(姓)
- fill in(= *out*) ~을 메우다; (서류) 에 적어 넣다, 필요한 항목을 써넣다
- fillet steak 안심스테이크
- first aid equipment 응급처치장비
- first name(= *given name*) 이름
- flat (맥주·사이다 등이)김빠진
- flavor 향미, 맛
- foyer 로비
- free child care center 무료 탁아방
- full milk 지방우유

G
- garlic 마늘
- get out of (접시, 기물 등을)치우다
- gin and tonic 진토닉
- glass 유리컵
- go through ~을 통과하다
- go 보내다

H
- have a reservation 예약을 하다
- have a table 좌석이 있다
- have dinner(*lunch, something to eat, etc.*) 저녁을 먹다
- hesitate 주저하다, 머뭇거리다, 망설이다
- high-speed 고속(도)의
- hold 수용하다
- hold on a second 잠깐만 기다리세요.
- housekeeper 하우스키퍼
- housekeeping 하우스키핑

I
- in advance 선금으로, 미리
- include 포함하다
- injure 상처를 입히다
- instruction 지시
- invoice 영수증
- ironing(=*pressing*) 다림질
- issue 문제점
- itemize 항목별로 쓰다, ~의 명세를 적다

K
- king prawn 왕새우

L
- license 면허
- lift(=*elevator*) 승강기
- lobster 바다가재
- look forward to + V-ing ~을 기대하다
- luggage stand 선반
- luggage(=*baggage*) 여행용 수화물

M
- machine 기계
- made from ~에서 만들다
- magnetic strip 신용카드 뒷면의 마그네틱
- make a phone call 전화를 걸다
- make a reservation 예약하다
- mean 의미하다
- medium 중간
- meeting room 회의실
- menu 메뉴, 식단표
- meringue 머랭(설탕과 거품 일게 한 흰자위 등을 섞은 것)
- method of payment 지불조건
- mid-afternoon
- mineral water 천연 광천수
- minibar (호텔 객실 등의) 주류 상비용 소형 냉장고
- mistake 잘못, 착오
- mushroom 버섯
- mussels 홍합

N
- N/A = not applicable
- name 성명
- nationality 국적
- nearby 가까이에, 근처에
- non-smoking room 금연 객실

O
- offer 제공하다
- on foot(*by bus / car / train / air*) 걸어서
- on the house 공짜로
- on the rocks 얼음만 넣은
- open 열다
- organize (행사 등을)준비 하다, 계획하다
- overcooked 너무 익힌(구운)

P
- pack (짐을) 꾸리다
- pain 고통
- panoramic 파노라마(식)의
- passport 여권
- past 지나쳐서
- pay 지불하다
- pay-per-view TV프로그램 유료 시청제
- pharmacist 약사
- pharmacy 약국
- photocopier 사진복사기
- pillow 베개
- place an order 주문하다
- porter 운반인
- pot 컵
- prawn 참새우
- pretty 매우
- projector 투사기
- pudding 푸딩
- purchase 구입하다

R
- rare 덜 구워진
- reach ~에 도착하다
- receipt 영수증
- regards (편지에서의) 안부 인사
- register 등록부
- registration 등록
- registration card 숙박 등록 카드
- reject 거절하다
- request 요청하다, 부탁하다
- restaurant 레스토랑, 음식점
- right away 곧바로
- rooftop 지붕, 옥상
- room no.(number) 객실번호
- room rate 객실요금
- room service 룸 서비스 (호텔에서 방으로 식사를 날라다 주는)

S
- safe 금고
- salmon 연어
- sandwich 샌드위치
- satellite TV 위성 TV
- sauce 소스, 양념
- scallops 가리비
- seat 좌석, 자리
- secretarial 비서(관)의
- secure 안전하게 하다
- send up 보내다
- separately 따로따로
- serve 접대하다, 주문을 받다

- server 서비스 제공자
- settle 놓다
- short-staffed 직원(요원)부족의
- show 보여주다
- side(=*side dish*) 곁들여 나오는 요리
- signature 서명
- slip 계산서 사본
- smell 냄새가 나다
- smoke 담배 피우다
- snack 간식, 스낵
- sorbet(=*sorbet*) 셔벗, 과즙 아이스크림
- sound 소리
- soup 수프
- sparkling 발포성의, 탄산성분이 들어간
- special board
- specify 명기하다
- spell 철자를 말하다
- split 분담하다
- standard 표준수칙
- state 주(州)
- stay 머무르다
- still 비발포성의, 탄산 성분이 들어가지 않은
- suit 슈트, 한 벌
- surname : 성
- swipe (카드를) 힘껏 긁다

T

- take 타다
- tart 타트, 파이
- terrible 굉장히
- theater 극장
- thermostat 자동 온도 조절 장치
- toast 토스트, 구운 빵
- toothache 치통
- toothbrush 칫솔
- transaction 처리, 거래
- travel agent 여행사
- traveller's check 여행자 수표
- trolley 트롤리
- trousers (남자용) 바지
- turn (right, left) (모퉁이를) 돌다

U

- undercook 덜 익다
- unload 짐을 내리다

V

- vacancy 빈방
- valuable 귀중품
- VAT(=*value added tax*) 부가가치세
- video conference 화상회의
- voucher 상품권, 바우처

W

- wait 기다리다
- wake-up call(=*morning call*) 모닝콜
- walk along ~을 따라서 걷다
- window table 창가 좌석
- wine list 포도주 목록
- with tax (=*tax included*) 세금 포함
- work 일

Z

- zip(=*zipper*) 지퍼
- zip(=*zip code, postal code*) 우편번호

Appendix. 2 Terms of Hotel & Restaurant

A

Adjoining Room(=*Side by Side Room*) : 객실이 같은 방향으로 복도에 나란히 있지만, 객실과 객실사이에 연결된 문이 없이 이어져 있는 객실

Advance : 객실을 예약할 때 대금의 일부를 사전에 지불하는 것

Amenity : 고객 서비스의 plus 개념으로 "부가적인 서비스 제공"을 의미한다. 객실 내에 무료로 제공되는 빗, 샴푸, 린스, 헤어캡, 구두닦이 천, 반짇고리 등이 해당되며, 고객이 가져가도 무방함.

Aperitif : 식전주, 식전반주

Appetizer : 전채 요리로 앙트레 전에 제공되며, 소량의 음식으로 짠맛이나 신맛을 사용하여 입맛을 돋우는 역할, 계절감이나 지방색을 드러낼 수 있는 재료를 사용하는 것이 좋음.

Available Room : 호텔이 판매 가능한 객실을 말하며, House Use Room, Repair Room을 제외한 객실 수

B

Baby Sitter : 호텔 투숙고객의 자녀를 고객의 요청에 의하여 돌봐주는 사람으로, 주로 House Keeping의 Maid가 돌봐 주고 시간당 요금을 받는 것이 일반적임.

Baggage : 고객이 소지하는 개인 소유물, 수하물

Baggage Down : 고객이 퇴숙시 객실로부터 전화 또는 직접 문의에 의하여 Poter 또는 Bellman이 고객의 짐을 호텔 현관으로 운반해주는 서비스

Baggage Stand : 호텔 객실 내에 있는 가구 중의 하나로 트렁크 및 비교적 큰 수화물을 올려놓을 수 있는 받침대

Bath Tub : 욕조, 목욕탕

Bathrobe : 목욕 가운

Bill : 호텔의 객실, 식음료, 기타 부대시설에서 쓰이고 있는 고객용 영수증

Book : 호텔을 이용하고자 하는 고객들에게 미리 예약을 받거나 판매하는 것

C

Check-In : 고객이 Front에 도착하여 고객의 인적사항을 요구하는 등록카드를 접수한 후, 그 고객을 정해진 객실로 친절히 안내하기까지의 모든 행위

Check-Out : 고객과의 마지막 접촉은 퇴숙으로, 고객이 객실을 비우고 객실열쇠를 반환하고 비용을 정산하고 호텔을 떠나는 것

Closet(*Wardrobe*) : 벽에 부착된 옷장

Complimentary(*Comp*) : 호텔에서 특별히 접대해야 할 고객이나 호텔의 판촉 촉진을 위하여 초청한 고객에 한하여 요금을 부과하지 않고 무료로 제공하는 것. 객실만 무료인 경우를 Comp. on Room(*Room only Comp*)이라고 하며, 객실, 식사가 무료인 경우를 Comp. on Room & Meal(*Room & Meal Comp*)이라고 하고, 모든 것이 무료인 경우는 Comp 또는 Full Comp.

Confirmation Slip : 호텔 객실을 예약한 고객에게 예약이 정확하게 이루어졌음을 알려주는 일종의 확인서. 투숙자명, 도착일, 출발일, 객실 종류 등의 필요한 사항을 기입하여 고객에게 예약 사항을 확인하게 함.

Croissant : 초생달 모양의 빵으로, 터키 국기 속에 그려진 초생달 모양을 빵으로 만들었다는 유래가 있다. 프랑스에서 이후 더 개발되었으며 일반적으로 아침 식사용 빵을 가리킴.

D

D.D.D.(*Direct Distance Dialing*) : 장거리 전화. 직접 다이얼 통화로 시 구역 밖의 지역에 전화

Dessert : 디저트는 보통 앙트레와 샐러드 다음에 제공되는데, 디저트에는 단맛, 과일류, 치즈 등이 있으며 감미류는 찬 것과 더운 것으로 구분

Dinner : 저녁 식사로, 내용이나 시간적으로 충분한 시간과 양질의 재료로 요리한 식사

Drapery : 창문에 달린 커튼으로, 빛이 통과할 수 없는 두꺼운 천으로 만들어짐.

Dry : 술의 맛을 의미하는 용어로 독하거나 쓴 맛을 표현하는 형용사, 반대로 달콤한 맛의 술은 Sweet.

Dust Bin(*Rubbish Bin*) = 쓰레기통

E

Entre : Main dish를 의미하며, 중간에 나오는 순서의 것으로 Middle Course를 말함. 고대에 정찬요리에 통째로 찜 구이한 조류요리가 식사의 처음 코스로 제공되었다고 하며, 처음의 요리라고 하여 Entry(입구)의 의미로 Entre의 뜻으로 쓰였고 요즘에는 메인요리를 의미하게 됨. 일반적으로 육류 요리로는 소, 송아지, 양, 돼지, 가금류(닭, 오리, 비둘기), 엽수류(노루, 사슴, 산토끼), 엽조류(꿩, 메추리) 등이 있음.

Executive Chef(= *Head Cook, Chef de Cusine*) : 모든 음식을 조리하고 준비하는 책임을 지고 있으며, 메뉴 개발 및 메뉴 구성 등이 주 업무이다. 조리장은 식음료 부문에 대한 전반적인 지식이 필수임.

Executive Floor : EFL은 "호텔 내의 호텔", "귀빈층"이라고 불리며, 잦은 해외출장, 바쁜 스케줄, 복잡한 사무업무를 수행하는 비즈니스맨들에게 보다 신속하고, 정확하며 차별화된 서비스를 제공하는 호텔 내의 특별층. Concierge가 상주하고 있으며, 항공 예약 및 스케줄 변경, 확인, 타 호텔 예약, 비서업무, 통역, 클럽 라운지, Express Check In & Out, 회의 등 세심한 Amenity를 제공하는 곳

Extra Bed : 객실에 정원 이상의 고객이 투숙할 때 또는 Family Plan으로 투숙시 임시로 투입되는 침대로 접는 식의 이동하기 편리한 Roll Away Bed를 말하며, 추가요금 또는 무료로 제공

F

Family Plan : 부모와 함께 동행한 14세 미만의 어린이에게 Extra Bed를 제공하며 추가요금은 적용하지 않음.

Foie Gras : 거위 간으로 만든 전채 요리로 캐비어, 송로버섯과 함께 세계 3대 진미 중 하나

Foyer : 호텔의 휴게실, 로비(lobby).

G

Garnish : 고명, 장식물. 먹을 수 있는 식재료로 음식물을 보기 좋게 장식하는 것

I

Invoice : 거래 품목의 표시와 청구의 기능을 갖으며, 거래당사자, 목적물, 거래가액, 부가가치 세액, 거래일자, 주문서의 일련번호 등을 표시

L

Lunch : 영국에서는 아침과 저녁 사이에 먹는 식사를 Luncheon이라고 하며, 미국에서는 12:00 이후에 간단하게 먹는 것을 Lunch라고 한다. 보통 Table D'hote 순서에 따라 3~4 코스가 제공되며 Soup, Entre, Dessert, Coffee 등으로 구성됨.

Lobster : 보리 새우과에 속하는 새우의 하나로 바다 밑바닥의 벌에서 서식함. 보통 산채로 삶아서 저장하였다가 요리

M

Maid Card : 객실 청소를 하는 중이라는 표시로 룸메이드가 청소를 하고 있는 문 옆이나 문의 손잡이에 걸어 놓음.

Maid Cart : 룸페이드가 객실 청소에 필요한 모든 비품을 담는 짐수레(카트)

Make Bed : 사용한 베드(Bed)의 Sheet를 갈아 끼우고 새로운 베드(Bed)로 만드는 행위

Make Up : 고객이 객실에 등록되어 있는 동안 침대의 린넨을 교환하거나 객실을 청소하고 정비 정돈이나 청소를 요하는 객실

Menu : 프랑스어로 Carte라고 불리나 현재 전 세계 공통어로 Menu가 사용된다. 우리나라에서는 차림표 식단이라고 함.

Mineral Water : 광천수로 칼슘, 인, 칼륨, 라디움, 염소, 마그네슘, 철 등의 무기질이 포함

Mini Bar : 객실 내의 냉장고에 간단한 주류나 음료를 구비하고 이를 고객이 객실 내에서 이용하는 일종의 Small Bar.

N

Napkin : 주로 양식을 먹을 때 가슴을 가리거나 무릎위에 펴 놓으며, 손이나 입을 닦기도 하는 수건이나 종이.

Non Smoking Room : 호텔을 이용하는 고객 중, 담배를 피우지 않는 고객을 위한 금연객실

O

Order Taker : 고객으로부터 각종 주문을 접수, 처리하는 업무를 주 업무로 하는 호텔 직원

P

Peeling : 껍질을 벗긴다는 뜻

Pillow : 베개는 딱딱한 것, 부드러운 것, 높은 것, 낮은 것 등이 있고, 내용물은 스폰지, 메밀껍질, 깃털 등이 있는데, 주로 호텔에서는 깃털 베개를 많이 사용함. Single Bed의 경우 2개, Double Bed의 경우는 4개를 준비함.

Pressing Service : 고객 세탁 서비스 중 다림질 서비스.

R

Rare : 육류를 요리할 때 색상과 촉감으로 그 익은 정도를 나타내는 용어 중 하나로 완전 날고기를 따뜻하게 데운 정도를 표시하는 용어 육류요리는 요리되는 정도에 따라 Rare, Medium-Rare, Medium, Medium-Well, Well Done 5단계로 구분

Receipt(=*bill*) : 고객에게 주는 영수증.

Registration : 숙박등록, 숙박 계약

Registration Card : 등록카드로 호텔 고객의 숙박절차로서 소정의 카드에 필요한 사항을 기재함. 호텔 이름, 주소, 카드 No. 고객의 성명, 주소, 객실번호, 요금, 도착시간, 출발 예정시간, 취급 계산원 성명 등이 포함

Reservation : 객실이나 부대시설의 영업장 등에서 미래시점의 서비스를 위해 미리 판매하는 것

Raspberry : 나무딸기 열매로 장미과에 속하는 낙엽관목. 딸기와 비슷하며 색깔은 검정, 빨강, 보라 3종류가 있고, 제리, 잼, 파이, 무스를 만드는데 이용

Recipe : 레시피. 제조법을 말하며, 조리나 칵테일에 있어 재료 배합의 기준량과 만드는 순서를 총칭

Room Maid : 호텔 고객에게 안전, 청결, 쾌적한 객실 상품을 판매, 제공하기 위하여 호텔의 모든 객실을 정리 정돈하는 호텔 직원

S

Sauternes : 소테른. 프랑스 보르도 지방의 지역으로 세계적으로 유명한 Sweet White Wine의 생산지.

Snack : 간단한 식사

Sommelier : 소믈리에. 와인 전문가로 와인을 고객으로부터 주문받고 직접 테이블에 서브하며, 와인 시음과 테이스팅을 하는 사람으로 요리와 적합한 와인을 추천해주고, 와인 창고 관리, 와인 진열 등의 업무를 수행

Station : 영업장에서 주어진 구역 내에 설치되어 고객에게 필요한 사항을 서비스하기 위해 준비해 놓은 기구

T

Tariff : 호텔이 공시하는 기본요금

Toll Free Telephone Line : 무료전화를 가리키는 말로, 호텔에서는 여행사나 호텔의 단골 고객을 대상으로 무료전화를 제공

Traveler Check : 여행자 수표로 일종의 자기앞 수표로, 여행시 현금 지참으로 인한 위험이나 불안감을 감소시키고 현금처럼 사용할 수 있는 장점이 있으며, 사용시 서명이 필요하므로 도난당하더라도 비교적 안전하고 위조의 가능성이 적음.

Trolley : 호텔에서 물건을 운반할 때 사용하는 것.

U

Utensil : 주방 및 바에서 사용되는 기물의 총칭

V

Vacancy : 객실이 만실이 아닌 상태로 판매 가능한 객실이 남아 있는 상태

Vermouth : 와인을 기조로 하여 약재를 가미한 혼성주의 일종. 백포도주가 기주로 사용되며, 여러 가지 약초들과 향료를 사용하고, 식전주나 칵테일의 부재료로 사용됨.

VIP(*Very Important Person*) : 국빈, 귀빈 등 중요한 고객으로 지명도가 높거나 특별한 주의 및 관심을 요하는 고객

Voucher : 고객이 여행사나 항공사에 Tour, 식사, 관광, 객실 등의 비용을 미리 지불한 뒤, 호텔에 요금 대신 지급 보증서나 증명서를 제출하고 호텔은 이를 근거로 여행사나 항공사에 해당 비용을 청구함.

W

Wake-Up Call(= *Morning Call*) : 고객으로부터 요청을 받아 전화에 의해 해당 고객의 객실로 전화벨을 신호로 잠을 깨워주는 서비스.

Walk-In Guest : 사전에 예약을 하지 않고 당일에 직접 방문하여 투숙하는 고객

저자약력

한천영
미국 Western Michigan University 대학원 언어학과 졸업(MA)
충남대학교 대학원 영어영문학과 졸업(Ph.D.)
성심외국어대학 관광통역학과, 호텔경영학과 교수
현 청운대학교 호텔관광대학 호텔경영컨벤션학과 교수

이금실
인하대학교 영어영문학과 졸업
세종대학교 대학원 호텔경영학과 졸업(경영학 석사)
Q.C.E. 'EBP & Intensive English Language Courses' 수료
UNLV 'Study Tour & Hospitality ESL Workshop' 수료
서울현대전문학교 관광외식산업학부 외래교수
현 비티엠써비스(주) 팀장
　한국관광대학 겸임교수
　혜전대학교 호텔관광경영과 외래교수

오선영
경희대학교 호텔관광경영과 박사수료
영산대학교, 부산경상대학, 영진전문대 외 다수 대학 출강
서울시청 문화월드컵 홍보추진반 통역서비스
시드니 올림픽 KOREAN CULTURE EXPO 근무
현 동서대학교 겸임교수

Hospitality English

2008년 9월 10일 초판 발행
2014년 3월 5일 2판 발행

지은이 한천영 · 이금실 · 오선영
펴낸이 유제구
펴낸곳 파워북
주소 서울 마포구 염리동 161-5
대동빌딩 4층
전화 (02) 730-1412
팩스 (02) 730-1410
등록 1997.1.1 제300-1997-13

정가 13,000원
ISBN 978-89-8160-107-2

잘못된 책은 바꿔드립니다.